VOLUME 8

NEW TESTAMENT

THE NEW COLLEGEVILLE BIBLE COMMENTARY

FIRST THESSALONIANS, PHILIPPIANS, SECOND THESSALONIANS, COLOSSIANS, EPHESIANS

Vincent M. Smiles

SERIES EDITOR

Daniel Durken, O.S.B.

LITURGICAL PRESS

Collegeville, Minnesota

www.litpress.org

Nihil obstat: Robert C. Harren, *Censor deputatus.*
Imprimatur: ✢ John F. Kinney, Bishop of St. Cloud, Minnesota, August 30, 2005.

Design by Ann Blattner.

Cover illustration: *Peter's Confession* (from Matthew 16) by Donald Jackson. Natural hand-ground ink on calfskin vellum, 15-7/8" X 24-1/2." Copyright 2005 *The Saint John's Bible* and the Hill Museum & Manuscript Library at Saint John's University, United States of America.

Photos: pages 10, 75, Corel Photos; pages 37, 55, 96, Jeffrey Hutson; page 111, David Manahan, O.S.B.

3	4	5	6	7	8	9

Library of Congress Cataloging-in-Publication Data

Smiles, Vincent M., 1949–
    First Thessalonians, Philippians, Second Thessalonians, Colossians, Ephesians / Vincent M. Smiles.
        p.   cm. — (The new Collegeville Bible commentary. New Testament ; v. 8)
        Summary: "Complete biblical texts with sound, scholarly based commentary that is written at a pastoral level; the Scripture translation is that of the New American Bible with Revised New Testament and Revised Psalms (1991)" —Provided by publisher.
        ISBN-13: 978-0-8146-2867-6 (pbk. : alk. paper)
        ISBN-10: 0-8146-2867-2 (pbk. : alk. paper)
        1. Bible. N.T. Thessalonians—Commentaries.   2. Bible. N.T. Philippians—Commentaries.   3. Bible. N.T. Colossians—Commentaries.   4. Bible. N.T. Ephesians—Commentaries.   I. Title.   II. Series.

BS2725.53.S65 2005
227'.077—dc22

                                                                    2005009782

CONTENTS

ABBREVIATIONS

Books of the Bible

Acts—Acts of the Apostles
Amos—Amos
Bar—Baruch
1 Chr—1 Chronicles
2 Chr—2 Chronicles
Col—Colossians
1 Cor—1 Corinthians
2 Cor—2 Corinthians
Dan—Daniel
Deut—Deuteronomy
Eccl (or Qoh)—Ecclesiastes
Eph—Ephesians
Esth—Esther
Exod—Exodus
Ezek—Ezekiel
Ezra—Ezra
Gal—Galatians
Gen—Genesis
Hab—Habakkuk
Hag—Haggai
Heb—Hebrews
Hos—Hosea
Isa—Isaiah
Jas—James
Jdt—Judith
Jer—Jeremiah
Job—Job
Joel—Joel
John—John
1 John—1 John
2 John—2 John
3 John—3 John
Jonah—Jonah
Josh—Joshua
Jude—Jude
Judg—Judges
1 Kgs—1 Kings

2 Kgs—2 Kings
Lam—Lamentations
Lev—Leviticus
Luke—Luke
1 Macc—1 Maccabees
2 Macc—2 Maccabees
Mal—Malachi
Mark—Mark
Matt—Matthew
Mic—Micah
Nah—Nahum
Neh—Nehemiah
Num—Numbers
Obad—Obadiah
1 Pet—1 Peter
2 Pet—2 Peter
Phil—Philippians
Phlm—Philemon
Prov—Proverbs
Ps(s)—Psalms
Rev—Revelation
Rom—Romans
Ruth—Ruth
1 Sam—1 Samuel
2 Sam—2 Samuel
Sir—Sirach
Song—Song of Songs
1 Thess—1 Thessalonians
2 Thess—2 Thessalonians
1 Tim—1 Timothy
2 Tim—2 Timothy
Titus—Titus
Tob—Tobit
Wis—Wisdom
Zech—Zechariah
Zeph—Zephaniah

INTRODUCTION

On his own admission, Paul once tried to destroy the church, but because of "a revelation of Jesus Christ" (Gal 1:11-16) he became in many respects the greatest of the apostles (1 Cor 15:8-10) and the most important witness of early Christianity. His conversion to become "an apostle of Christ Jesus" (1 Cor 1:1) happened about three years after Jesus' death (c. A.D. 33); he then worked as an apostle for about thirty years, until his own death in Rome during the persecutions of Nero (c. A.D. 64).

By far the most important source for knowledge of Paul is his own letters. The Acts of the Apostles, written by the same author as the Gospel of Luke, also provides an important history, but "history" in the modern sense of the term, that is, having a strong focus on factual information, was not Luke's primary purpose. As in the Gospel, Luke's *primary* concerns were theological, to provide "assurance" about Jesus' life, death, and resurrection (Luke 1:4; Acts 2:36).

Neither Luke nor Paul knew Jesus personally. It is *possible* that Luke knew Paul personally, as the famous "we" passages in Acts suggest (Acts 16:10-17; 20:5-8, 13-15; 21:1-18; 27:1–28:16). However, those passages may be stylistic devices rather than proof of eyewitness participation in Paul's ministry, and in various ways Luke seems *not* to have known Paul well: his letters are never mentioned or quoted, his attitude to the law and his Pharisaic past (Gal 3:1-29; Phil 3:2-6) are not understood (e.g., Acts 23:6; 26:5), and Luke has Paul in Jerusalem more frequently than Paul's own report allows (Acts 9:23-26; 11:27-30; 12:25; 15:1; cf. Gal 1–2). Therefore, though Acts is valuable, Paul's own letters remain the decisive source for knowledge of his ministry.

There are thirteen letters that bear Paul's name, and the letter to the Hebrews has also been attributed to Paul, but that was doubted as early as Origen (about A.D. 200), and today there is virtual consensus that Paul had no role in its composition. Of the thirteen, there is general agreement that Paul wrote Romans, 1 and 2 Corinthians, Galatians, Philippians, 1 Thessalonians, and Philemon. The other six letters divide into two groups: Ephesians, Colossians, and 2 Thessalonians, which in the view of *most* scholars Paul probably did not write, and 1 and 2 Timothy and Titus (the Pastoral Letters), which *nearly all* scholars believe Paul did not write. Reasons for doubting Paul's authorship of Ephesians, Colossians, and 2 Thessalonians will be given in the introductions to those letters. Authorship, however, is a complex matter. Paul wrote in the name of his co-workers (e.g., Timothy and Silvanus), indicating their support for the letter. When others wrote in his name, they did so because of some connection, however remote, with his authority and tradition.

Paul's original seven letters (epistles) were written between the late forties and early sixties A.D., *before* any of the four Gospels (A.D. 65 to 90). The letters are very *circumstantial,* meaning that Paul composed them to respond to particular situations that he and his churches faced. That is why his letters are such valuable witnesses of early Christianity. Interpretation of the letters must always take these circumstances into account. This is also true, for the most part, of the letters that Paul probably did not write. Ephesians is the exception in that it appears to be a general treatise on the church, written with a broad audience in mind rather than a particular community. Colossians and 2 Thessalonians, however, were composed in light of real problems facing churches that looked to Paul as *"the* apostle," as he was known to later generations. The authors wrote in Paul's name because it evoked great authority and trust.

The most important circumstance of Paul's time that we must bear in mind was his presumption that the end of human history (the *eschaton*) was at hand (see 1 Cor 7:29-31). Although later he was not so sure (Phil 1:20-24), early in his ministry Paul was convinced that he would be alive at "the coming of the Lord" (1 Thess 4:15). When "with the voice of an archangel and with the trumpet of God" the Lord Jesus himself would "descend from heaven," Paul expected that he would be among those "still alive," who would be "caught up together" with the dead "to meet the Lord in the air" (1 Thess 4:15-17). From such texts (e.g., also Mark 13:26-27; Matt 24:40-41), some modern Christians have developed the notion of "the rapture," and have combined it with the presumption that Paul and the evangelists were not talking about expectations of the first century but about the end of the world in the twentieth, and now twenty-first, century.

This is naïve, not to say shallow and self-serving, interpretation. How can we presume that Paul wrote primarily for us today? What about the people to whom he actually wrote, not to mention all the centuries in between? A full reading of the letters shows that Paul and his later disciples wrote entirely for the people and circumstances of their own time. The Scriptures are relevant today because the theologies, principles, and values they enunciate are foundational for the church in every age. Taking texts out of context and isolating chosen ideas for literal fulfillment today (what about the dragon of Revelation 12:3-4?) does no justice to the intentions of the biblical authors. That Paul and others were wrong about the near end of the world is only another indication that the Scriptures, like Jesus, have to do with "the weak flesh of humanity" as well as with the divine Spirit of inspiration (see Vatican II, Dogmatic Constitution on Divine Revelation, art. 13).

The value of Paul's letters for the church today is as great as the challenges the church faces. For questions of doctrine and morality, in debates about the nature of the church and of ministry, and facing questions about evangelization and mission, the church now, as always, has to turn to Jesus and to the church's original foundation and inspiration. Paul is particularly important as the witness of how the earliest churches first enfleshed the gospel of Jesus. His descriptions of the church, particularly as "the body of Christ" (1 Cor 12:27); his instructions about the Eucharist (1 Cor 10–11) and inclusion of women among church leaders (e.g., Rom 16:1-7); his recounting of major incidents (Gal 1:13–2:14); and his christological understanding (e.g., Phil 2:6-11)—these and many other aspects of his letters, and of the letters written in his name, are primary texts for the church today. The best approach to the letters requires prayer, an open mind, and careful study both of their individuality and of the conversation, and sometimes vigorous debate, that together they represent.

The following historical framework is suggested for the five letters in this commentary:

33	Paul's conversion
	First visit as an apostle to Jerusalem (Gal 1:18-19)
	Ministry in Arabia, Cyprus (?), Antioch and cities of Asia Minor
48	The Council of Jerusalem (Gal 2:1-10; Acts 15)
	Ministry in Asia Minor and Greece (Antioch as base)
49	—*1 Thessalonians* (from Corinth)
	Ministry in Asia Minor and Greece (Ephesus as base)
55–56	—*Philippians* (from Ephesus)
	Last visit to Jerusalem and arrest there (Acts 21)
64	Paul's death in Rome
66–70	—*Colossians* (from Ephesus by someone close to Paul)
80–90	—*Ephesians*
90s	—*2 Thessalonians*

Introduction

The commentaries in this booklet are all primarily based on the Greek text rather than the New American Bible translation. Accordingly, the translation of words or phrases in the commentaries sometimes differs from the translation provided at the top of the page. It is hoped that these complementary translations will enhance understanding of the letters.

The First Letter to the Thessalonians

The importance of I Thessalonians, and its place and date of writing

The First Letter to the Thessalonians is the earliest of all the New Testament writings. It was probably composed in Corinth—perhaps Athens—in A.D. 49 or maybe even earlier (41–44?). Thirteen letters bear Paul's name; of them, scholars agree that Paul wrote at least seven (Romans, 1–2 Corinthians, Galatians, Philippians, 1 Thessalonians, Philemon); the authenticity of each of the others (Ephesians, Colossians, 2 Thessalonians, 1–2 Timothy, Titus) is disputed. Paul was martyred (probably) in Rome in the early sixties; he wrote all his letters, therefore, before any of the Gospels were written (Mark—c. 70—being the first Gospel). This makes Paul the earliest witness of Christianity, and 1 Thessalonians the earliest part of Paul's testimony.

Thessalonica (modern-day Thessaloniki or Salonika) is located at the far northwestern end of the Aegean Sea. In Paul's time it was the principal city of the Roman province of Macedonia. According to the more traditional reconstruction of his apostolic journeys (following the outline of the Acts of the Apostles), Paul ventured into Macedonia and Achaia (Greece) in the late forties, after a long ministry in Syria and Asia Minor that was based in Antioch (c. 34–48). It is possible, however—some think probable—that he began his westward journeys earlier, reaching Greece as early as 41. Whatever the date, he arrived there from Philippi (1 Thess 2:2; Acts 16:11–17:1) and subsequently traveled south to Beroea (Veria), Athens, and Corinth (1 Thess 3:1; Acts 17:10–18:1).

The evidence of Acts

As indicated, Acts also recounts these travels, but there is not always complete consistency between Acts and Paul's own letters. Acts was written about twenty years after Paul's death (about 85) and is primarily a *theological* narrative about the early church. It contains some valuable historical

information, but exact history is not its primary purpose. In the case of Paul's mission in Thessalonica, there are some clear contrasts between Acts and 1 Thessalonians: Acts 17 (a) has Paul in Thessalonica only three weeks; (b) envisions mostly Jewish converts; and (c) does not mention Timothy being in Thessalonica. The letter, however, (a) implies a more substantial stay than three sabbath sermons (2:9; see also Phil 4:16); (b) envisions a mostly Gentile community (1:9, "turned from idols"); and (c) makes clear that Timothy was a primary missionary (1:1; 3:2-6). In all cases the letter to the Thessalonians, written by an eyewitness, is to be preferred over Acts, which is an important but secondary source. Acts, therefore, is not a major help either in reconstructing this part of Paul's history or in understanding the letter. While not dismissing Acts, interpreters of Paul must focus *primarily* on the texts of his letters.

The occasion and purpose of I Thessalonians

Fortunately, 1 Thessalonians provides valuable clues to its context, and its purpose is substantially clear. Paul, Silvanus, and Timothy had labored long and hard in Thessalonica (2:9) and had successfully established house-churches there (5:27), which yet were sufficiently united that Paul could refer to them as "the church of the Thessalonians" (1:1). The letter does not say why the "apostles" (2:7) left Thessalonica, but given the letter's focus on "affliction" (1:6; 3:3-7), it probably had to do with local opposition (2:14); in this regard Acts 17:5-9 may well be correct. In other words, the missionaries probably left before they wanted to. Paul, then, was anxious about this fledgling church; would they be able to persevere?

In Athens the apostles decided that Timothy must return "to find out about [their] faith" (3:5). The news he brought back elated Paul, and he set about writing this letter of thanksgiving and encouragement. Timothy also seems to have relayed to Paul some questions and concerns, both from the Thessalonians themselves and, perhaps, from his own observations. Most notably, they seem to have asked about whether believers who had died would be included in the resurrection of the dead (4:13-18). There may also have been questions about marriage (sex?—4:3-7), and some members of the community may have been faltering in their commitment to Christ (5:14). It must be said, however, that detecting real problems behind Paul's advice is extremely difficult; not every exhortation from Paul necessarily corresponds to some issue among the readers.

Does I Thessalonians comprise one letter or two?

Such reconstructions of what was going on in Thessalonica become all the more tenuous when we take into account the views of some experts

11

that 1 Thessalonians actually comprises more than one letter. The theory goes that 1 Thessalonians 2:13–4:2 was originally a separate (earlier) letter, written shortly after Paul had left Thessalonica, and that when Paul's letters were gathered together, this shorter letter was incorporated into the "second letter," comprising 1:1–2:12 and 4:3–5:28. The strongest argument in favor of this theory is the second "thanksgiving," which begins in 2:13. This is unique among the letters certainly written by Paul (cf. 2 Thess 2:13). There is also some tension between 2:6-7, which suggests some lapse of time since Paul's founding visit, and 2:17, which speaks of being absent from Thessalonica "for a short time."

These arguments cannot lightly be dismissed, but they have not convinced most scholars who continue to take the letter *mostly* as it is. "Mostly" signals a problem, and the problem is 2:13-16, particularly 2:14-16. The latter three verses, which feature very harsh language against "the Jews who killed the Lord Jesus," have been debated vigorously for many years. As the commentary will show, there are substantial reasons for thinking that they (along with 2:13?) may have been added to the letter in the late first century.

Again, however, most scholars are not convinced of this. The policy adopted here is to acknowledge the weight of these important questions about the letter's integrity, but nevertheless to interpret the text as it has come to us from ancient tradition. The minority view may yet prove to be correct, but for now the weight of the evidence is that 1 Thessalonians has come to us essentially as Paul wrote it.

The importance of I Thessalonians for the church today

For the life of the church, this is by far the most important question. The letter's history is essential for a basic understanding of what the letter *meant* to its first audience, but it is because of what the letter *means* today that believers still read it. Historical study is essential to a modern reading, but it is not the whole of it. Present meaning, however, is largely determined by present questions and concerns; every generation will hear somewhat differently based on its circumstances. The following are some obvious themes that are important for the church today.

1. *The church as a local community:* In spite of the Second Vatican Council (e.g., the Dogmatic Constitution on the Church), "the church" today still connotes, for a large number of believers, the institutional church and the hierarchy. For Paul and the New Testament as a whole, there was no such connotation. In those days "the church" meant everything from a house-church (e.g., Rom 16:5; Gal 1:2) to that whole collection

of "the churches" that had been established in various cities of the Roman Empire (see 2 Cor 8:24; Col 1:24). Paul's authentic letters are all addressed to the men and women of the community, whether Thessalonica, Corinth, or elsewhere. This was true whether the community was to be praised for its faith (e.g., 1 Thessalonians, Philippians) or corrected for its abuse of the Eucharist (1 Cor 11:17-34) or some other fault. "The church of the Thessalonians" had its leaders (see 5:12-13), but Paul's primary concern was "the church," from which its leadership and ministry arose.

2. *Leadership in the church:* Male, ordained clergy have dominated leadership in the church for so many centuries that modern readers inevitably read the New Testament as though it presupposed the same structure. This, however, is not the case. We know nothing specific about the leaders whom Paul mentions in 1 Thessalonians 5:12-13, but from Paul's other letters we know that women were included among the primary leaders of the churches (see Rom 16:1-7; Phil 4:2-3; Col 4:15). And though Acts (14:23) says that Paul "appointed presbyters in each church," in the authentic letters "presbyters" are never mentioned. Ministry in Paul's churches did not primarily depend on "appointment" (ordination) but on the charisms of the Spirit (1 Cor 12). This means that structures of ministry, even today, are susceptible to change.

3. *The ongoing power of the gospel:* Finally, it should be noted that Paul was vividly aware of the *presence* of God's action in believers' lives and of the ongoing power of the gospel. After so many centuries of history, believers have a tendency to look to the past as the source of inspiration and revelation. This, of course, is correct as far as it goes, but it misses Paul's emphasis that the word of God "*is now* at work" among believers (1 Thess 2:13), that "*now* is the day of salvation" (2 Cor 6:2). The inspiration of the Bible is to be found not only in its writers but also in its readers.

The First Letter
to the Thessalonians

I. Address

1 **Greeting.** [1]Paul, Silvanus, and Timothy to the church of the Thessalonians in God the Father and the Lord Jesus Christ: grace to you and peace.

Thanksgiving for Their Faith. [2]We give thanks to God always for all of you, remembering you in our prayers, unceasingly [3]calling to mind your work of faith and labor of love and endurance in hope of our Lord Jesus

---

1:1 Greeting

Paul associates Silvanus and Timothy (Acts 16:1-3) with himself in the writing of the letter. Silvanus ("Silas" in Acts) was from Jerusalem; Paul met him there at the conference (about A.D. 48) when the status of Gentiles in the church was discussed (Acts 15:1-27). Subsequently, he replaced Barnabas as Paul's traveling companion after Paul and Barnabas had a disagreement (15:36-40). He then traveled with Paul through Asia Minor and assisted in establishing churches in Galatia (16:6), Philippi (16:11-29), Thessalonica (17:1-4), and Corinth (18:5; 2 Cor 1:19). After Corinth he is no longer mentioned in association with Paul, but 1 Peter 5:12 associates him with Peter and the writing of that letter.

Timothy was extremely important to Paul (see Phil 2:19-23). It was Timothy whom Paul sent back to Thessalonica to find out how the church was doing (1 Thess 3:2, 5); that "sending" confirms that Paul was the leader of the team. Timothy joined Paul's mission shortly after Silas (Acts 16:1-3) and then remained throughout Paul's apostolate (Rom 16:21; Acts 20:4), probably until the imprisonment that ended with Paul's death in Rome. Though the letter speaks throughout in terms of "we" (except 3:5; 5:27), there is no reason to doubt that Paul is the primary and perhaps the sole author of the letter. Nevertheless, the collaborative nature of his leadership is important to note, and it may, in part, help to explain why his

Christ, before our God and Father, ⁴knowing, brothers loved by God, how you were chosen. ⁵For our gospel did not come to you in word alone, but also in power and in the holy Spirit and [with] much conviction. You know what sort of people we were [among] you for your sake. ⁶And you became imitators of us and of the Lord, receiving the word in great affliction, with joy

---

companions and successors felt free, after his death, to write letters in his name (e.g., Ephesians, Colossians, 2 Thessalonians).

The addressee is "the church of the Thessalonians." We should envisage a house-church or several of them (5:27), a fairly small community by modern standards. "Church" in the New Testament always designates a community of people, whether a house-church (e.g., Rom 16:3-5; Acts 2:46), the believers of a city (1 Cor 1:2), or the church as a worldwide community (Eph 1:22-23); it never designates an abstract institution, nor is it ever identified simply with its leadership. The church exists "*in* God the Father and the Lord Jesus Christ." The greeting is brief (cf. Rom 1:7; 1 Cor 1:3), with "grace" *(charis)* being an especially important term for Paul—a near one-word summary of his gospel (Rom 5:15-21; 11:6; 1 Cor 15:10; Gal 1:6; 5:4). Paul inserts *charis* ("grace") where standard Greek letters had *chairein* ("greetings"), and he adds "peace" (Hebrew *shalom*), perhaps reflecting a greeting found in Jewish letters.

1:2-10 Thankful remembrance of preaching in Thessalonica

This is similar to the "thanksgiving" sections of Paul's other letters (e.g., Rom 1:8-15; 1 Cor 1:4-9; Phil 1:3-11), but here he is particularly enthusiastic and joyful, because in spite of persecution (1:6; 2:14; 3:6-8), they have persevered in the "work of faith, the labor of love, and the endurance of hope" (1:3). This triad (faith, love, hope) is recalled later (5:8: "the breastplate of faith and love, helmet of hope"). In fact, a major reason for the letter is Paul's desire to encourage them in faith and love, but most especially in hope, in the face of persecution and the death of loved ones (4:13-18). Paul recalls here their positive reception of "the gospel" (1:5) and reminds them of their "election" and that they are "loved by God" (1:4).

Election, more commonly referred to as God's "call," is a key idea in Paul's letters (see Rom 9:7-26; 11:26; 1 Cor 7:18-24), this one in particular (2:12; 4:7; 5:24). It is the starting point for much of Paul's theology, pointing as it does to God's initiative of love and grace. The election takes place

from the holy Spirit, ⁷so that you became a model for all the believers in
Macedonia and in Achaia. ⁸For from
you the word of the Lord has sounded
forth not only in Macedonia and [in]
Achaia, but in every place your faith in
God has gone forth, so that we have no
need to say anything. ⁹For they themselves openly declare about us what
sort of reception we had among you,

---

apart from human expectation or calculation (see Rom 5:6-8: "while we
were sinners"), and indeed, even "apart from the law" (Rom 3:21). The
Thessalonians "knew *that*" (rather than *how*) they "were chosen" in "the
gospel" that Paul and his companions preached (1:5).

"Gospel" in the New Testament never refers to a book, nor does it refer
to any particular doctrines. It refers simply to the *act* of proclamation,
which was not "in word alone" but was a matter of "power" and "the
holy Spirit" and "conviction" (1:5). For Paul, the gospel always has about
it immediacy and living power; it happens "today" (2 Cor 6:2: "*now* is the
day of salvation") and has powerful effects. In other words, *God enables*
faith (Phil 1:29) and the "knowing of election" (1:4); behind true preaching
there is always the loving action of God.

The effect among the Thessalonians was that they "became imitators
of [the apostles] and of the Lord" both in "affliction" and in "joy" (1:6).
More than that, they became "a model" for believers throughout the
region. Their gracious "reception" of the apostles became legendary, so
that others reported how the Thessalonians "turned from idols to serve
the living and true God" (1:8-9). The abandonment of traditional religions
was one of the most difficult and amazing acts of ancient believers. In the
context of modern freedoms, it is difficult to appreciate that such "turning" required great courage, since it inevitably caused social disruptions,
even in families (1 Cor 7:12-15; Luke 12:51-53: "father against son, son
against father") and was the source of persecution both from locals (2:14;
Acts 17:5-9) and, ultimately, from the Romans.

Verse 10 explains their motivation. It is an important verse, since it is
the earliest summary of what believers preached and believed. "Awaiting
[God's] Son from heaven" points to the very apocalyptic atmosphere of
early Christian experience. Paul and others expected to be "alive" at "the
coming of the Lord" (4:15), which is also described as "the coming wrath"
(1:10). But for believers this will not mean "condemnation" (Rom 8:1), but
rather "rescue" at the hands of God's resurrected "Son." How and when
Jesus will come again is an important issue in 1 Thessalonians (2:19; 3:13;
4:13–5:11; 5:23), but later it recedes in importance (e.g., in Ephesians).

and how you turned to God from idols
to serve the living and true God ¹⁰and
to await his Son from heaven, whom
he raised from [the] dead, Jesus, who
delivers us from the coming wrath.

II. Previous Relations
with the Thessalonians

2 **Paul's Ministry Among Them.** ¹For
you yourselves know, brothers, that
our reception among you was not without effect. ²Rather, after we had suffered
and been insolently treated, as you

know, in Philippi, we drew courage
through our God to speak to you the
gospel of God with much struggle.
³Our exhortation was not from delu-
sion or impure motives, nor did it work
through deception. ⁴But as we were
judged worthy by God to be entrusted
with the gospel, that is how we speak,
not as trying to please human beings,
but rather God, who judges our hearts.
⁵Nor, indeed, did we ever appear with
flattering speech, as you know, or with
a pretext for greed—God is witness—

Such expectation, however—a vibrant awareness of the nearness of
God—holds rich vitality for spiritual life and should not simply be dismissed as outdated. Investments in this world (marriage, business) have
their own goodness, but their value is better seen in the light of the world
to come, "for the framework of this world [and all our investments] is
passing away" (1 Cor 7:31).

2:1-12 Paul's defense of the apostles' preaching in Thessalonica

As already in 1:4 Paul addresses the community as "brothers," but this
does not mean he intends the letter only for men; the term *adelphoi* is best
translated "believers." Paul presupposed the patriarchal culture of his
world (e.g., 4:4; 1 Cor 11:2-16: "husband, the head of his wife," 11:3), but
he also knew that "in Christ" such patriarchy has no place (Gal 3:26-28:
"no longer male and female" in Christ), and, to some extent, working
with women in leadership, he did overcome patriarchal biases. It is
inaccurate, therefore, to portray Paul as a misogynist; the evidence that
women worked with him in his apostolic labors is unmistakable (e.g.,
Rom 16:1-7, 12-15: Phoebe, Prisca, Junia; Phil 4:2-3: Euodia, Syntyche).

Paul turns to a defense of the apostles' behavior while in Thessalonica.
"Defense" suggests there had been accusations, but there is no direct evidence of this. Elsewhere Paul, when attacked, was not shy about directly
rebuffing his detractors (2 Cor 10–13; Gal 2:11-14). In Thessalonians, for

▶ This symbol indicates a cross reference number in the *Catechism of the Catholic Church*. See
page 123 for number citations.

[6]nor did we seek praise from human beings, either from you or from others, [7]although we were able to impose our weight as apostles of Christ. Rather, we were gentle among you, as a nursing mother cares for her children. [8]With such affection for you, we were determined to share with you not only the gospel of God, but our very selves as well, so dearly beloved had you become to us. [9]You recall, brothers, our toil and drudgery. Working night and day in order not to burden any of you, we proclaimed to you the gospel of God. [10]You are witnesses, and so is God, how devoutly and justly and blamelessly we behaved toward you believers. [11]As you know, we treated each one of you as a father treats his children, [12]exhorting and encouraging you and insisting

some reason, Paul fears being thought of as one of those preachers of his time who represented themselves as experts in some religion and traveled around making money from their converts. He acknowledged that apostles had the right to material support (1 Cor 9:3-7), but he also knew of Christian preachers who, in his view, were greedy "peddlers of the word of God" (2 Cor 2:17) and whom he contrasted with himself in his preaching of the gospel "without charge" (2 Cor 11:7; 1 Cor 9:12).

Paul had come to Thessalonica by way of Philippi, where he also had encountered opposition (2:2). In reminding the Thessalonians of his conduct, he says five times what it did *not* involve: deception, people-pleasing, flattery, greed, and being a (financial) burden (2:5-9). It's a veritable catalog of what preachers should avoid. It was rather a matter, "through our God" (2:2), of great "struggle," of "toil and drudgery, working night and day, in order not to burden any of you" (2:9). "As apostles of Christ, we could," he says, "have imposed our weight, but we were gentle [or 'infants'] among you, like a nursing mother cherishing her children" (2:7). It is interesting here to recall Jesus' words: "Among the nations those who are seen as rulers over the Gentiles lord it over them. . . . But it shall not be so among you. Rather, whoever wishes to be great among you will be your servant" (Mark 10:42-43). Paul's actual conduct accords with Jesus' instruction.

In 2:11 Paul changes the image, comparing Silvanus, Timothy, and himself to a "father, exhorting and encouraging each one as his own children." Against any possible detractors, Paul insists that their conduct was devout, just, and blameless (2:10) as they taught the community that their conduct also must be "worthy of the God who [even now] calls [them] into his kingdom" (2:12). It is important to note the *present* tense—the gospel is not a thing of the past.

that you conduct yourselves as worthy of the God who calls you into his kingdom and glory.

Further Thanksgiving. [13]And for this reason we too give thanks to God unceasingly, that, in receiving the word of God from hearing us, you received not a human word but, as it truly is, the word of God, which is now at work in you who believe. [14]For you, brothers, have become imitators of the churches of God that are in Judea in Christ Jesus. For you suffer the same things from your compatriots as they did from the Jews, [15]who killed both the Lord Jesus and the prophets and persecuted us;

2:13-16 Four problematic verses

This paragraph, especially verses 14-16, is much disputed in modern scholarship, the dispute being whether this generalizing and harsh condemnation of "the Jews" is authentic or was added later in light of persecution by Jews (e.g., John 16:2) and the destruction of Jerusalem by the Romans in A.D. 70. Paul's letters were indeed collected and edited. Second Corinthians, for instance, may be a conflation of at least two letters to Corinth (2 Cor 1–9 and 10–13), and 1 Corinthians 14:33b-36 may be an editorial addition to that letter. However, here, as also in those cases, the ancient manuscripts are as they are, and scholars, no matter what their convictions, cannot cut and paste the Bible as they choose.

The evidence that 2:(13?)14-16 is a later addition has some weight:

1. It does not fit well into the flow of the letter, much less into the sequence of Paul's ministry. "God's wrath has come upon them" (2:16) does not fit well into this early period; it might fit better after Jerusalem was destroyed in A.D. 70.

2. It contains some (for Paul) unusual ideas (e.g., that Jews were responsible for Jesus' death; cf. 1 Cor 2:8, where "rulers of this world" does *not* designate Jews).

3. It seems harshly anti-Jewish, especially in light of Paul's affection for his heritage (e.g., Rom 9:1-5: "I could wish that I myself were accursed for the sake of my people"; 11:1-2).

On the other hand, the arguments in favor of its authenticity are also persuasive:

1. All ancient manuscripts contain the passage.

2. Its unusual features may derive from the use of traditional language by Paul (cf. Luke 11:47-51).

19

they do not please God, and are opposed to everyone, [16]trying to prevent us from speaking to the Gentiles that they may be saved, thus constantly filling up the measure of their sins. But the wrath of God has finally begun to come upon them.

Paul's Recent Travel Plans. [17]Brothers, when we were bereft of you for a short time, in person, not in heart, we

---

3. The critique is not *anti*-Jewish so much as *intra*-Jewish, not unlike the harsh words of the prophets (e.g., Jer 7:33-34) or Jesus (Matt 23:29-33).

4. Though he loved his heritage, Paul was quite capable of harsh critique of Jews with whom he disagreed (see Rom 2:17-24). In the presence of such uncertainty, it is foolish to be dogmatic one way or the other, though the case for authenticity does seem slightly stronger.

As the letter stands, 2:13 accords well with the theme of 1:5, namely, that the gospel, though proclaimed by human agency, ultimately derives its power from the "word of God, which is now at work in you who believe." "Word of God" here does not mean words *about* God, but rather the word that *God speaks* now, in every generation, the word that "is active and alive" (Heb 4:12). Paul's angry language in 2:14-16 gives no warrant whatsoever to anti-Semitism and, in some respects, is rather questionable. The primary responsibility for the death of Jesus lay with the Roman authorities, crucifixion being a Roman punishment. And the accusations that Jews "do not please God and are opposed to everyone" (2:15) are more reflective of the anti-Jewish propaganda of ancient authors than of the esteem for Jews that Paul elsewhere demonstrates.

The horror of Christians using Scripture to justify unspeakable cruelty toward innocent people must be forever rejected. If Paul did indeed write these words, he intended to assure the Thessalonians that they were suffering just like "the churches of God in Judea" (2:14), and his anger no doubt derived, in part, from the harsh treatment that he received in some synagogues (2 Cor 11:24: "five times I received thirty-nine lashes from the Jews"). But his very accepting of that punishment witnesses that he remained connected to Judaism. He longed for Jews to accept the gospel (Rom 9:1-3; 10:1), and he lived out his belief that "the gifts and call of God" to Israel "are irrevocable" (Rom 11:29).

2:17–3:13 The difficulty and the joy of recent events

Paul now resumes his expressions of affection and longing for the Thessalonians. Such emotional outpouring may seem strange today. His

were all the more eager in our great desire to see you in person. [18]We decided to go to you—I, Paul, not only once but more than once—yet Satan thwarted us. [19]For what is our hope or joy or crown to boast of in the presence of our Lord Jesus at his coming if not you yourselves? [20]For you are our glory and joy.

[3] [1]That is why, when we could bear it no longer, we decided to remain alone in Athens [2]and sent Timothy, our brother and co-worker for God in the gospel of Christ, to strengthen and encourage you in your faith, [3]so that no one be disturbed in these afflictions. For you yourselves know that we are destined for this. [4]For even when we

---

language, in part, is conventional—he also tells believers in Rome that he "long[s] to see" them (Rom 1:11), though he had never even met them; he calls the Philippians also his "joy and crown" (Phil 4:1), and he tells the Corinthians (2 Cor 1:14) and Philippians (Phil 2:16) as well as the Thessalonians that they will be his "boast at the coming of the Lord" (2:19).

But convention alone does not explain his language. The range of strong emotions in Paul's letters is considerable—joy, gratitude (Phil 4:10-14); rage (Gal 3:1; 5:12!); outrage (2 Cor 11:13-15); sorrow (2 Cor 2:1-4); and exhilaration (Phil 4:4-7). The list could go on. But for all his churches, even when he was angry at them (Gal 4:19-20), he clearly held a sincere affection (2 Cor 11:11: ". . . because I do not love you? God knows that I do!").

That affection is nowhere more evident than here. Away from Thessalonica, the apostles felt "orphaned" (2:17). Paul himself had tried twice to return to them, "but Satan prevented us" (2:18). Satan is mentioned again in 3:5 as "the tempter" who might do harm to the community's faith. In both cases Paul may have seen "Satan" in the political opposition which he himself had encountered in Thessalonica (see Acts 17:6-7) and which now harassed the believers and prevented Paul's return. This forced separation, whatever its cause, became completely unbearable for Paul, and while in Athens they determined that Timothy must return to find out whether the Thessalonians' faith was holding up under the pressure (3:1, 5). Why Timothy could make the journey and Paul could not is impossible to answer. Timothy's mission was "to strengthen and encourage" and especially to see to it that "no one was disturbed" by the persecutions and other "afflictions" they were enduring (3:2-3). Paul had warned them that suffering is inevitable in the life of faith, and now they have experienced it for themselves (3:4).

"Just now," however—as though he had just walked through the door!—Timothy has brought "the good news of [their] faith and love,"

21

were among you, we used to warn you in advance that we would undergo affliction, just as has happened, as you know. ⁵For this reason, when I too could bear it no longer, I sent to learn about your faith, for fear that somehow the tempter had put you to the test and our toil might come to nothing.

⁶But just now Timothy has returned to us from you, bringing us the good news of your faith and love, and that you always think kindly of us and long to see us as we long to see you. ⁷Because of this, we have been reassured about you, brothers, in our every distress and affliction, through your faith. ⁸For we now live, if you stand firm in the Lord.

Concluding Thanksgiving and Prayer. ⁹What thanksgiving, then, can we render to God for you, for all the joy

---

and Paul, suffering some distress of his own (whether in Athens or, more likely, Corinth), is "consoled by [their] faith" (3:6-7). Indeed, for him this good news of their "standing in the Lord" is "life" itself (3:8). It may be significant that though Timothy recounted their "faith and love," he could not speak of their "hope" (1:3; 5:8). It has been suggested that "hope" was the one thing that was "lacking in [their] faith" (3:10), and that may well have been. Harassment from other citizens and the death of loved ones (4:13) must have been a heavy burden. Whatever the circumstances, the Thessalonians were enduring well, and Paul now simply breaks into prayer, wondering what "thanksgiving" he can possibly render for the joy he feels on their account (3:9).

What he comes up with are two petitions. Predictably, he prays first that "God and our Lord Jesus" will make it possible for himself, Silvanus, and Timothy to visit Thessalonica soon (3:10-11). His second prayer is addressed to "the Lord" (Jesus) alone, a telling indication of how closely, even in the earliest theological reflection, Jesus was identified with God. He prays that Jesus will "increase [their] love" and "strengthen [their] hearts" to be "blameless" at his "coming with all his holy ones" (3:12).

What Paul means by "holy ones" is not immediately obvious. We naturally think of angels (Matt 16:27), and that may well be correct, but elsewhere Paul never mentions angels or "holy ones" (saints) at the Lord's coming. For Paul, "holy ones" always refers to *believers* (e.g., Rom 1:7; 12:13; 15:25-26); he regularly addresses his letters (this one being the exception) "to the saints" of Rome, Corinth, and so on. But the language Paul uses here is traditional; he quotes from Zechariah 14:5, which speaks of God's coming "and all his holy ones with him." The tradition Paul employs, therefore, certainly envisions angels, as also most probably Paul himself does. It would be nice to think that Paul has in mind the believers

we feel on your account before our God? ¹⁰Night and day we pray beyond measure to see you in person and to remedy the deficiencies of your faith. ¹¹Now may God himself, our Father, and our Lord Jesus direct our way to you, ¹²and may the Lord make you increase and abound in love for one another and for all, just as we have for you, ¹³so as to strengthen your hearts,

to be blameless in holiness before our God and Father at the coming of our Lord Jesus with all his holy ones. [Amen.]

III. Specific Exhortations

General Exhortations. ¹Finally, brothers, we earnestly ask and exhort you in the Lord Jesus that, as you received from us how you should con-

---

of Thessalonica who have died (4:13; note 4:14b), but 4:16 says "they will rise" when the Lord "will descend from heaven." The whole picture is a further reminder of the deeply apocalyptic character of this letter and of early Christian experience in general.

4:1-12 Exhortation to holiness

Just as the thanksgiving in this letter is inordinately extended, so also are the exhortations to good behavior, this being the first such section, 5:12-22 the second. Extended exhortation, however, is not unusual for Paul (Rom 12:1–13:14; Gal 5:13–6:10) and makes sense, given his aim of "strengthening" in this letter.

There are several difficulties for interpreters, most especially in verses 3-6. The biggest problem is the interpretation of verse 4, which very literally reads: ". . . that each of you know how to obtain (control?) his vessel in holiness." All agree that this metaphor ("vessel") has to do with proper sexual conduct, but does Paul mean (a) to obtain a *wife* or (b) generally to control *sexual behavior*? The first option (as in the New American Bible) is not popular these days, but that, of course, is not a reason to reject it. It is also *possible* that Paul is referring to, and forbidding, consanguineous marriages (Lev 18:6-18), which Greek society permitted in order to keep the woman's inheritance in the family. If this is the case, then the injunction "not to exploit a brother in this matter" (4:6) refers to the business contract involved in transferring the woman's property to her husband. In any event, 4:3-7 almost certainly intends to warn the Thessalonians against sexual "impurity"; the latter word, in Paul, regularly refers to sexual misconduct (e.g., Rom 1:24; Gal 5:19).

The alternative is that both men and women are being told to "control [their] sexual behavior" and that 4:6 either reinforces this by forbidding any sexual irregularities or, perhaps (but less likely), introduces the differ-

duct yourselves to please God—and as you are conducting yourselves—you do so even more. ²For you know what instructions we gave you through the Lord Jesus.

Holiness in Sexual Conduct. ³This is the will of God, your holiness: that you refrain from immorality, ⁴that each of you know how to acquire a wife for himself in holiness and honor, ⁵not in lustful passion as do the Gentiles who do not know God; ⁶not to take advantage of or exploit a brother in this matter, for the Lord is an avenger in all these things, as we told you before and solemnly affirmed. ⁷For God did not call us to impurity but to holiness.

⁸Therefore, whoever disregards this, disregards not a human being but God, who [also] gives his holy Spirit to you.

Mutual Charity. ⁹On the subject of mutual charity you have no need for anyone to write you, for you yourselves have been taught by God to love one another. ¹⁰Indeed, you do this for all the brothers throughout Macedonia. Nevertheless we urge you, brothers, to progress even more, ¹¹and to aspire to live a tranquil life, to mind your own affairs, and to work with your [own] hands, as we instructed you, ¹²that you may conduct yourselves properly toward outsiders and not depend on anyone.

---

ent issue of justice in business practices ("do not defraud"). Overall the first option ("obtain a wife"), whether we like it or not, seems more likely. If this is correct, then this is one of those texts where Paul's, and his society's, patriarchal biases show (cf. 1 Cor 11:2-16), and modern believers are not bound to first-century cultural standards. In any event, believers are not called to "uncleanness," a general term for various types of immorality (2:3), but to "holiness" (3:13).

Paul speaks here—and 4:8 strongly confirms this—as one who represents Christ ("in the Lord"), so that to ignore him is tantamount to "ignoring God" (cf. Luke 10:16). Paul was always adamant that his apostolic authority derived from God (Gal 1:6-12); it was not, he acknowledged, from official channels and was not always recognized by others (1 Cor 9:2); it was nevertheless real and effective (1 Cor 15:10). "The will of God" for the Thessalonians is their "holiness" (4:3-4), by which he means that they are to live by "the holy Spirit that God gives [them]" (4:8; again, note the present tense). "Holiness" (4:7) is not primarily something to be attained, as though they did not have it, but is a gift they are to practice. Already, he says, they know his instructions—they are "God-taught"—and he has no need to tell them about love, which they practice "toward all the believers" (4:9-10). He concludes the section by urging them to "live quietly, mind [their] own business, and work with [their] own hands" so as to provide for their needs and be on good terms with outsiders (4:11-12).

Hope for the Christian Dead. ¹³We do not want you to be unaware, brothers, about those who have fallen asleep, so that you may not grieve like the rest, who have no hope. ¹⁴For if we believe that Jesus died and rose, so too will God, through Jesus, bring with him those who have fallen asleep. ¹⁵Indeed, we tell you this, on the word of the Lord, that we who are alive, who are left until the coming of the Lord, will surely not precede those who have fallen asleep. ¹⁶For the Lord himself, with a word of command, with the voice of an archangel and with the trumpet of God, will come down from heaven, and the dead in Christ will rise first. ¹⁷Then we who are alive, who are left, will be caught up together with them in the clouds to meet the Lord in

4:13-18 The hope of faith in the face of death

This is one of the most fascinating apocalyptic texts in the entire New Testament and, for study purposes, should be compared with similar texts (e.g., Mark 13; Matt 24; Rev 21). We learn here that Paul and his contemporaries expected Jesus' second coming in the very near future, and, indeed, Paul expected to be "alive" for the event (4:15). By the time he wrote Philippians 1:21-24 (six to ten years later), he could anticipate that he might be dead before the end, but a vivid expectation of Jesus' return never left him.

Occasionally, believers are disconcerted at the early church's "mistake" in expecting Jesus to return "soon" (Rev 1:1-3), and critics sometimes make it a basis for discrediting Christian faith. Imminent expectation was not, however, foundational to faith. The delay of the end did, understandably, disturb some early believers (2 Pet 3:3-10), but then as now faith's primary focus was on being "God's children" and on living out that reality in the here and now.

The pressing circumstance in Thessalonica, about which the Thessalonians had probably questioned Timothy, was the death of some of their loved ones; would they also "be with the Lord" at his coming (4:14, 17)? Paul is interestingly inconsistent in his answer: 4:14b ("God *will bring* [them] *with* Jesus") does not quite jibe with 4:16 ("the dead in Christ *will arise*" *at his descent* "from heaven"). This slight confusion reminds us not to be too caught up in the details of what will happen at the end; there are many differing descriptions in the New Testament.

The point Paul makes is that believers' grief should be tempered by the hope of the resurrection and the awareness that God is very near. The basis of this hope is the power of Jesus' death and resurrection (see 1 Cor 15:12-19). That power reaches beyond death, so that those "who are left

the air. Thus we shall always be with the Lord. [18]Therefore, console one another with these words.

5 **Vigilance.** [1]Concerning times and seasons, brothers, you have no need for anything to be written to you. [2]For you yourselves know very well that the day of the Lord will come like a thief at night. [3]When people are saying, "Peace and security," then sudden disaster comes upon them, like labor pains upon a pregnant woman, and they will not escape.

[4]But you, brothers, are not in darkness, for that day to overtake you like a thief. [5]For all of you are children of the

alive at the Lord's coming" will have no advantage over "the dead in Christ" (4:15). God will "take up" the living and "raise up" the dead, and "thus we shall always be with the Lord" (4:16-17).

Modern readers of 4:17 ("we will be caught up with them in the clouds") need to beware of fundamentalist interpretations which insist that this text foretells a very literal "rapture" (snatching up) of Christians into heaven at the end of the world. Those who interpret the text this way often also insist that "these are the last days," as though they had some knowledge denied to everyone else. Mark 13:32 insists to the contrary that "no one—not the angels, not even the Son—knows that day or hour." Paul, like Jesus (Matt 24:40-41), used the imagery of apocalyptic literature in accordance with the culture of his time; but believers are bound by faith, not by particular cultural ideas, whether of marriage (4:4; Col 3:18, "wives, be subordinate"), slavery (Col 3:22, "slaves, obey your masters"), or apocalypticism. Bumper stickers that claim, "When the Rapture comes, you take the wheel!" are cute at best; at worst, they are a serious misreading of Scripture, not to say arrogant. Paul's major point, speaking to believers grieving at the death of loved ones, is that God is very close to the living and the dead, both now and in eternity.

5:1-11 Further instructions about the coming end

The apocalyptic atmosphere continues unabated in this next section, with Paul suggesting (as in 4:1-2, 9) that the Thessalonians know everything he might tell them about "times and seasons." Evidently this was already discussed at some length when he, Silvanus, and Timothy were with them. The imagery Paul uses ("thief in the night," "birth pangs") is also found in other apocalyptic texts, both Christian (Matt 25:43; Mark 13:8) and Jewish (1 Enoch 62:4), and "the day of the Lord" recalls prophetic texts of God's coming judgment (Joel 2:1; Amos 5:18-20). Paul's point here is that believers have nothing to fear; they are "children of light

light and children of the day. We are not of the night or of darkness. ⁶Therefore, let us not sleep as the rest do, but let us stay alert and sober. ⁷Those who sleep go to sleep at night, and those who are drunk get drunk at night. ⁸But since we are of the day, let us be sober, putting on the breastplate of faith and love and the helmet that is hope for salvation. ⁹For God did not destine us for wrath, but to gain salvation through our Lord Jesus Christ, ¹⁰who died for us, so that whether we are awake or asleep we may live together with him. ¹¹Therefore, encourage one another and build one another up, as indeed you do.

---

and the day" and so live by a different code than "the rest" of the world that are "in darkness" (5:4-6).

We encounter here the dualism of apocalyptic thinking, namely, the idea that "we, who are being saved" stand over against "them, who are perishing" (1 Cor 1:18; 2 Thess 2:10). The division of time into "this age" and "the age to come," and of humanity into the "saved" and the "lost," was a regular feature of apocalypticism long before the time of Jesus (e.g., Dan 12:1-3). To this day, such language convinces some Christians that outside of Christian faith there is no salvation, but the question of whether unbelievers can be saved is answered both in Scripture (Matt 25:31-46) and in church teaching (Dogmatic Constitution on the Church, art. 16) with a clear yes. Paul, to be sure, thought that unbelievers were headed for "the coming wrath" (1:10), but in this, as in other things, believers must exercise discernment, relying not only on Scripture but also on God-given intelligence, on the guidance of the Spirit, church tradition, and, as Vatican II reminds us, "the secular sciences" (The Church in the Modern World, art. 62).

The strength of Scripture is in the great principles it enunciates of love and justice and its revelation that all people are created "in God's image" and are God's children. A strict application of the Bible's laws and its pronouncements of judgment has never served the church well. Paul's knowledge of the world and history was far more restricted than ours, as also therefore was his context. It is essential that we keep these things in view as we evaluate Paul's text.

For their part, believers are to avoid idle carousing; they are to be clothed with faith, love, and hope as they await the fullness of salvation (5:8-9). Paul recalls again Jesus' "dying for us," which is the basis of Christian hope (5:10; see 4:14). Paul, in fact, recalls the power of that death over and over in his letters (e.g., Rom 3:25; 4:25; 14:9; 1 Cor 1:18-25; Gal 2:19-21). It binds us to God, so that "whether we live or die," there is no separation (5:10).

Church Order. [12]We ask you, brothers, to respect those who are laboring among you and who are over you in the Lord and who admonish you, [13]and to show esteem for them with special love on account of their work. Be at peace among yourselves.

[14]We urge you, brothers, admonish the idle, cheer the fainthearted, support the weak, be patient with all. [15]See that no one returns evil for evil; rather, always seek what is good [both] for each other and for all. [16]Rejoice always. [17]Pray without ceasing. [18]In all circumstances give

5:12-22 Final instructions and exhortations

The exhortations here are universal in scope, applicable to any church in any age. And yet they witness to essential, fundamental truths of faith about both church order and Christian morality. In 5:12-13 we have the earliest text ever on church leadership. Paul addresses the entire community, asking them to "acknowledge those who labor among you." These were the women and men who functioned as primary leaders by virtue of their spiritual gifts and faith-commitment. The presumption of some that women were not church leaders has to do with our patriarchal history and bias, not with historical accuracy. The Pontifical Biblical Commission acknowledged already in 1976 that "some women collaborated in *the properly apostolic work*" and named Prisca (Rom 16:5), Euodia and Syntyche (Phil 4:2-3), Phoebe and Junia (Rom 16:1-2, 7) as examples. Paul urges the church to hold such people in high esteem and to show them love. And that is all; leaders are essential, but the task of ministry belongs fundamentally to the church as the body of Christ (1 Cor 12:7, "to each is given the manifestation of the Spirit for the common good").

Having described the leaders as "those who admonish (instruct) you," Paul goes on to tell the whole community to "admonish the disorderly" (not "the idle," though note 2 Thess 3:6-12). He may have a specific problem in mind here, but what that was we cannot know. The same is true regarding the commands to "encourage the fainthearted [and] support the weak" (5:14). Perhaps these are believers who are timid in the face of persecution. Whatever the case, it is the task of the church to support them. It is also everyone's responsibility to "ensure that no one repays evil for evil"; they are rather to seek the good of all, including outsiders (5:15; cf. 4:12).

The series of rapid-fire commands that follows in 5:16-22 reads like poetry; only the added sentence in 5:18 ("this is God's will for you in Christ Jesus") disturbs the rhythm and rhyme of the Greek text. Theology and spirituality can be much enriched by meditation on these exhortations. In spite of all the hardships that so preoccupy this letter, Paul insists

thanks, for this is the will of God for you in Christ Jesus. ¹⁹Do not quench the Spirit. ²⁰Do not despise prophetic utterances. ²¹Test everything; retain what is good. ²²Refrain from every kind of evil.

Concluding Prayer. ²³May the God of peace himself make you perfectly holy and may you entirely, spirit, soul, and body, be preserved blameless for the coming of our Lord Jesus Christ.

²⁴The one who calls you is faithful, and he will also accomplish it. ²⁵Brothers, pray for us [too].

IV. Final Greeting

²⁶Greet all the brothers with a holy kiss. ²⁷I adjure you by the Lord that this letter be read to all the brothers. ²⁸The grace of our Lord Jesus Christ be with you.

that believers "rejoice always, pray unceasingly, in every circumstance give thanks." The charismatic character of early Christianity is apparent in the command not to "extinguish the Spirit," the Spirit being envisaged as a flaming fire (cf. Acts 2:3, "tongues as of fire"). A primary gift of the Spirit was prophecy, which, though much valued by Paul (1 Cor 14:1-5, 29-33), was subject to abuse and therefore required discernment (5:21). Paul's concern for the church's public image is again apparent in the final command, "Avoid every appearance of evil" (5:22).

5:23-28 Final greeting and blessing

Finally, Paul once again breaks into prayer (cf. 4:11-13) and, once again, the "holiness" and "blamelessness" of the Thessalonians are what he requests (5:23). Their sanctification to the point of being "perfect" is not something they can accomplish of themselves, and thus Paul asks God to accomplish this in them. "Holiness" is not primarily a human endeavor (cf. 4:3). The prayer looks forward to "the coming of our Lord Jesus Christ," when their divinely gifted integrity of "body, mind and spirit" will be apparent. The "God who calls [them] is faithful and will accomplish this" (5:24).

Paul asks for their prayers and, as elsewhere, he instructs them to greet one another "with a holy kiss" (5:26; Rom 16:16; 1 Cor 16:20; cf. 1 Pet 5:14). He then solemnly puts them on oath to "make sure the letter is read to all the believers" (5:27), meaning probably that there were several house-churches within the church of Thessalonica, as was also true in other places (Gal 1:2; Col 4:15). His final blessing is the same as at the end of all his letters. Its fullest form, which we still use today at the beginning of our liturgies, is found in 2 Corinthians 13:13, and as was the case at the beginning, he wishes them "the grace of our Lord Jesus Christ." So ends the very earliest piece of Christian literature—a powerful witness of what the church was and is always to be, a *community* of "faith, love and hope" (1:3; 5:8).

The Letter to the Philippians

The importance of Philippi

Philippi was located about 110 miles northeast of Thessalonica in Macedonia. It got its name in 360 B.C. from Philip II of Macedon, father of Alexander the Great. In 42 B.C. it was the scene of a great battle to decide the successor of Julius Caesar; Caesar Augustus, the emperor at the time of Jesus' birth, was the victor. In 31 B.C. he made Philippi a Roman colony, permitting army veterans to settle there. Philippi, therefore, enjoyed special status; it came under Italian law and was exempt from various taxes. Paul was aware of its prestige (see 3:20; 4:22).

According to Acts 16:9, a vision summoned Paul to preach the gospel in Macedonia. From the very beginning Paul's relations with Philippi were warm and affectionate; it was the one church that consistently supported him in his apostolic work (4:15-16, cf. 1:5). Its founding members and leaders included a number of women (4:2-3; Acts 16:13-15), but unlike other cities of Paul's mission, Philippi seems not to have included a synagogue or any large Jewish population. The issue of when and where Paul wrote his letter to the Philippians takes us into its particular difficulties.

Challenges for interpretation

Scholars are agreed that Paul wrote Philippians, but most also believe that the letter we have was originally two or three separate letters. The most obvious seam is between 3:1 and 3:2; the switch of mood is so abrupt that even those who defend the unity of the letter struggle to explain the transition. Another difficulty is the delayed thank-you (4:10-20), which interrupts what looks like a standard ending of a letter (4:8-9, 21-23).

These and other observations have given rise to numerous theories about the original *letters* to Philippi and, of course, such theories affect the question of when and where Paul wrote. A common theory of multiple letters regards 4:10-20 as *letter A*, written from prison in Ephesus, about A.D. 55. *Letter B*, from prison a few weeks later, comprises 1:1–3:1a, 4:4-7, 21-23, and *letter C* includes the polemical 3:1b–4:3, 8-9 after Paul's release and was written perhaps from another city (Corinth?). A more simple theory would be: *letter A* = 1:1–3:1; 4:1-7, 10-23 (from Ephesus, about 55), and *letter B* = 3:2-21; 4:8-9 (from Corinth, about 56). All such theories presuppose that an editor, for some reason, conflated the original two or three letters and in doing so chopped off the openings and endings of one or more letters to avoid needless repetition.

Those who reject such theories insist that, in spite of difficulties, the letter is coherent and should be read as a unity, and certainly it *can* be read as a unity. The commentary to follow will do so, without denying that the theories of division are, at least from a historical perspective, very valuable. Assuming its unity, where was Paul when he wrote Philippians? The traditional view is that he wrote from Rome in the early sixties while under house arrest (Acts 28:16-31). Philippians, however (see 1:12-20; 2:17), envisions more than house arrest, and travel between Rome and Philippi was more difficult than the ease of communication that is presumed in the letter (2:19-30). Some scholars think Ephesus was the more likely place of writing, some time in the mid-fifties. There is no explicit record of Paul being imprisoned in Ephesus, but that is not an insurmountable problem (see 2 Cor 1:8; 11:23; 1 Cor 15:32). The best guess, therefore, is that Philippians comprises one or more letters written from prison in Ephesus in the mid-fifties and perhaps also from Corinth a year or so later.

The Letter to the Philippians

I. Address

1 **Greeting.** [1]Paul and Timothy, slaves of Christ Jesus, to all the holy ones in Christ Jesus who are in Philippi, with the overseers and ministers: [2]grace to you and peace from God our Father and the Lord Jesus Christ.

Thanksgiving. [3]I give thanks to my God at every remembrance of you, [4]praying always with joy in my every prayer for all of you, [5]because of your partnership for the gospel from the first day until now. [6]I am confident of this, that the one who began a good work in

1:1-2 Greeting

The opening is brief and simple but includes interesting details. Timothy is named as co-sender, but he probably had little to do with the actual composition of the letter. From 1:3 Paul speaks in terms of his particular experience (e.g., 1:12-17); this letter, like the others that are original to Paul (Romans, 1 and 2 Corinthians, Galatians, Philippians, 1 Thessalonians, Philemon), bears the imprint of one very strong personality. It is unusual that Paul here does not claim the title "apostle." It was sometimes important for him to do so (e.g., Rom 1:1; Gal 1:1-12), but in the warm relationship he shared with Philippi, there was no such need. "Slaves" recalls Jesus' instruction about leadership (Mark 10:44).

Even more interesting, but also strange, is Paul's special mention of "the overseers and ministers." The Greek terms (*episkopos* and *diakonos*) are sometimes translated "bishop" and "deacon" (e.g., 1 Tim 3:2, 8), but in his list of primary church functions (1 Cor 12:28), these titles have no place, and in fact "overseers" are never mentioned again in the original letters. He uses "minister" (*diakonos*) to describe, among others, himself and other leading "ministers" of the gospel (1 Cor 3:5; 2 Cor 3:6), but only in the case of Phoebe (Rom 16:1) does it have an official ring to it. These titles are so unusual that some scholars think the phrase was inserted by an editor, but this is doubtful. They must have been leaders of various house-churches—people like Euodia, Syntyche, and Clement (4:2-3).

▶ This symbol indicates a cross reference number in the *Catechism of the Catholic Church*. See page 123 for number citations.

33

you will continue to complete it until
the day of Christ Jesus. ⁷It is right that I
should think this way about all of you,
because I hold you in my heart, you
who are all partners with me in grace,
both in my imprisonment and in the
defense and confirmation of the gospel.
⁸For God is my witness, how I long for

The letter is addressed to *"all* the holy ones" (the baptized); he greets
them with the standard but significant formula he employs in all his
letters: "Grace to you and peace . . ." Though Paul addresses the community six times as "brothers" (e.g., 1:12), it is important to note that he is
addressing women and men alike (note 4:2-3). *Adelphoi* ("brothers") in
this context is best translated "believers."

1:3-11 The thanksgiving

The warmth of Paul's relationship with the Philippians is evident here:
"I thank my God at *every* remembrance of you, praying *always* with joy at
my *every* prayer for *all* of you." In Greek the italicized words all begin
with the letter "p," increasing the emotional and rhetorical effect. "My
God" (also 4:19; Rom 1:8) denotes a personal relationship and is quite
common in the psalms (e.g., Ps 22). "Joy" characterizes this letter throughout (1:18; 2:2, 17; 3:1; 4:1, 4, 10).

As a "thanksgiving," the passage is a standard feature of letter writing
(cf. Rom 1:8-15; 1 Cor 1:4-9, etc.), but there is nothing standard or merely
formal about Paul's "joyful" remembrance of the Philippians and of their
"partnership in the gospel from the first day until now" (1:5). "Partnership"
(or "participation"—see 2:1; 3:10; 4:15) refers both to their spiritual and
their material sharing in the task of the gospel (see 4:15). They "defend
and confirm" (1:7) the gospel by living it and by "struggling together" for
its progress (1:27). They have also generously enabled Paul's missionary
endeavors by their gifts to him (4:16); the phrase "until now" may refer to
Paul's having just received their latest contribution.

The beginning of the "good work" that God "will continue" in them
was that "first day," when Paul came to Philippi and was received, according to Acts 16:11-15, by Lydia and the other women at the "place of prayer."
Lydia herself is not mentioned in Philippians, but the leadership of women
seems to have remained important (4:2-3) in the intervening years. Lydia
was from Thyatira (northwest Asia Minor), says Luke (Acts 16:14), so she
may no longer have been in Philippi.

The "day of Christ" is the first of several references to the expected
return of Jesus (see 1:10; 2:16; 3:20-21). Some years earlier Paul had fully

all of you with the affection of Christ Jesus. ⁹And this is my prayer: that your love may increase ever more and more in knowledge and every kind of perception, ¹⁰to discern what is of value, so that you may be pure and blameless for the day of Christ, ¹¹filled with the fruit of righteousness that comes through Jesus Christ for the glory and praise of God.

II. Progress of the Gospel

¹²I want you to know, brothers, that my situation has turned out rather to advance the gospel, ¹³so that my im-

prisonment has become well known in Christ throughout the whole praetorium and to all the rest, ¹⁴and so that the majority of the brothers, having taken encouragement in the Lord from my imprisonment, dare more than ever to proclaim the word fearlessly.

¹⁵Of course, some preach Christ from envy and rivalry, others from good will. ¹⁶The latter act out of love, aware that I am here for the defense of the gospel; ¹⁷the former proclaim Christ out of selfish ambition, not from pure motives, thinking that they will cause me trouble in my imprisonment. ¹⁸What difference

expected to be alive for Jesus' return (1 Thess 4:15-17), but now he realizes that he may die first (1:20-23). Nevertheless, the end will come soon, and Paul's confident prayer (1:9) is that, at the judgment, the believers of Philippi will be "pure and blameless" (1:10). In the meantime, he says, he "longs for them with the affection of Christ Jesus" (1:8); Paul's love for his churches was unmistakable (1 Thess 2:7-8; 2 Cor 11:11). His final prayer is that they "will be filled with the fruit of righteousness" (1:11). Paul will resume this theme of "righteousness through Christ" in the fiery words of 3:2-9.

Although he was in prison (1:7, 13-17), the apostle was joyful and confident. Epaphroditus, who has delivered the Philippians' gift (4:18), remains with Paul, recovering, we will discover later, from a near brush with death (2:25-30). Also with Paul is Timothy, of whom Paul will speak affectionately (2:22).

1:12-26 The irresistible progress of the gospel

The first paragraph here (1:12-18) is remarkable, speaking as it does of the effect of Paul's imprisonment, first among "the praetorium and all the rest" (1:13), probably denoting non-believers, and second, among believers also (1:14-18). "The praetorium" (palace guard) refers not to a place but to the soldiers and others of "Caesar's household" (4:22). Paul wants the Philippians to know that his imprisonment, although on the surface a disadvantage, "served to advance the gospel." This goes along with Paul's optimistic tone, in spite of the most difficult circumstances. Even among

does it make, as long as in every way, whether in pretense or in truth, Christ is being proclaimed? And in that I rejoice.

Indeed I shall continue to rejoice, [19]for I know that this will result in deliverance for me through your prayers and support from the Spirit of Jesus

---

non-believers it has become known that Paul's imprisonment is "in Christ," meaning that they see Paul, not as a common criminal, but as a witness of Christ. And "most of the believers," far from being intimidated by his imprisonment, have gained greater confidence "to speak the word fearlessly" (1:14).

It is amazing that Paul has such equanimity in the circumstances he describes next. "Some," he says, "proclaim Christ because of envy and rivalry" (1:15), "thinking to cause me trouble in my imprisonment" (1:17). We know, then, that these opponents were Christians, but it is impossible to know much else about them or what sort of "trouble" (or "affliction") they might cause for Paul. Because he was a champion of the freedom of Gentile believers from the Jewish law, Paul ran into opposition many times, including in Antioch, Jerusalem (Gal 2:1-14; Acts 15:1-5), Galatia (Gal 1:6-9; 6:12-16), and Philippi (Phil 3:2-9; cf. Rom 3:8; 6:1-15).

The "trouble" these people sought to cause was perhaps simply distress in Paul's own mind. Their intention, however, may have been even more sinister, hoping to make his imprisonment worse and more protracted. Whatever the case, Paul refused to see it as a defeat. There was no trouble that could subdue his joy and confidence in Christ! Especially encouraging for him are those believers who preach Christ "for the sake of God's will" (1:15, not merely human "good will") and "out of love," aware that Paul was in prison "in defense of the gospel" (1:16). All that matters for Paul, whether to his advantage or not, is that "Christ is proclaimed; in that," he says, "I rejoice"!

"And I will continue to rejoice," he insists, "because I know that 'this will result in deliverance for me.'" These last words are from the book of Job (13:16). Whether or not the Philippians would recognize the reference—Philippians is almost devoid of Old Testament quotations—it seems clear that Paul sees in Job's words a reason for confidence. In the text in question, Job rebukes his friends because they have presumed to speak for God. Job, however, is convinced that they do not understand God's ways and that God, somehow, will vindicate him and bring him "deliverance" (or "salvation"). In applying this text to himself, Paul appears to be saying that he "knows" what will happen to him. In reality, however, he

36

Ruins of the three-aisled Basilica B in Philippi, dated to ca. A.D. 550

Christ. ²⁰My eager expectation and hope is that I shall not be put to shame in any way, but that with all boldness, now as always, Christ will be magnified in my body, whether by life or by death. ²¹For to me life is Christ, and death is gain. ²²If I go on living in the flesh, that means fruitful labor for me. And I do not know which I shall choose. ²³I am caught between the two. I long to depart this life and be with Christ, [for] that is far better. ²⁴Yet that I remain [in] the flesh is more necessary for your benefit. ²⁵And this I know with confidence, that I shall remain and continue in the service of all of you for your progress and joy in the faith, ²⁶so that your boasting in Christ Jesus may

---

does not even know whether the outcome will be "life or death" (1:20). Either alternative will be "deliverance"!

"The prayer" of his friends in Philippi and the "support of the Spirit of Jesus Christ" (1:19) are further reasons that Paul is confident. In fact, his confidence extends to "eager expectation and hope" (1:20). "Hope" here denotes the biblical virtue that "waits with eager longing" (Rom 8:19); it is not to be understood, as so often in modern speech, as a vague and anxious desire ("I hope the weather will be nice"). Paul fully "expects" his hope to be fulfilled. "I shall not be put to shame," he says, "in any way," meaning that there is nothing his enemies can do to defeat him. That is true for the simple reason that Paul has let go of any personal gain or advantage; all that matters is that "Christ is glorified," and whether that happens by Paul's "life or death" (1:20), it is all he desires.

Indifference to death is difficult to understand. We associate such indifference with the depths of despair and pain, but here it arises in a letter which, more than any other, exudes hope and joy. This gives a glimpse into Paul's spirit and into what motivated his long and difficult ministry. For Paul, "life" itself is nothing other than "Christ," and therefore "to die is gain" (1:21). To the Galatians he had said, "I have been crucified with Christ. I no longer live, rather, Christ lives within me" (Gal 2:19-20; cf. Rom 8:10-11). His entire life and identity are enfolded in his allegiance to Jesus. He is, therefore, content "to live in the flesh" for the sake of "fruitful labor" (1:22) for the gospel. On the other hand, he has a great desire "to depart this life and be with Christ—which is far better" (1:23). Nevertheless, he knows that it may be "more necessary for [their] benefit" to remain (1:24) and, for some reason, he seems convinced that this is the more likely outcome.

In fact, Paul is sure that he will "remain and abide with" them for their "progress and joy in the faith" (1:25), "so that" the Philippians "may boast in Christ Jesus" when Paul comes to them again. "Boasting" is closely re-

abound on account of me when I come to you again.

III. Instructions for the Community

Steadfastness in Faith. [27]Only, conduct yourselves in a way worthy of the gospel of Christ, so that, whether I come and see you or am absent, I may hear news of you, that you are standing firm in one spirit, with one mind struggling together for the faith of the gospel, [28]not intimidated in any way by your opponents. This is proof to them of destruction, but of your salvation. And this is

---

lated to the joyful hope that so fills this letter. Paradoxically, there is no such thing for Paul as "boasting" (Rom 3:27; 4:2; 1 Cor 1:29), as though humans could somehow be independent of God. On the other hand, within the relationship of faith, Paul often speaks of the joyful boast that believers can have because of what God enables within them (e.g., Rom 5:2-3; 2 Cor 1:12-14; Phil 2:16; 1 Thess 2:19).

1:27–2:18 Encouragement and instructions

Paul now changes his tone. In a long, complex sentence (vv. 27-30), he turns emphatically to instruction: "Only [one thing]—conduct yourselves worthily . . ." "Conduct yourselves" could be translated "be citizens" (cf. 3:20) and would be relevant in Philippi, which, as a Roman colony, was proud of its full citizenship rights. Believers, however, now are citizens under "Christ's gospel," and Paul's wish is that whether he can "come and see" them or not (2:12), he should "hear about" them that they "stand in one spirit" (1:27). "Spirit" might include reference to the Holy Spirit, but the parallel phrase "one mind" shows that Paul is primarily thinking of the spiritual unity of believers. "The faith of the gospel" (1:27) is a unique phrase; it probably means "the faith that arises from the gospel." Though the Philippians are being persecuted, they are not to "be startled in any way by the opponents" (1:28), the latter referring probably to unbelievers, the probable source of the trouble Paul himself experienced in Philippi (1 Thess 2:2).

The next part of this complex sentence gets even more difficult. "This," he says, "is proof to them of destruction, but of your salvation" (1:28). "This" must refer to the whole situation of belief opposed by unbelief. The next two phrases ("proof to them of destruction, but of your salvation") could mean (1) that unbelievers think that the outcome will be "destruction" for the church, with Paul, however, assuring believers that in reality it will be their "salvation." Alternatively, (2) Paul assures the church that the present situation shows that unbelievers are bound for destruction (cf. 1 Cor 1:18; 2 Cor 4:3), but believers for salvation (1:28; cf. Rom 8:28).

God's doing. [29]For to you has been granted, for the sake of Christ, not only to believe in him but also to suffer for him. [30]Yours is the same struggle as you saw in me and now hear about me.

2 **Plea for Unity and Humility.** [1]If there is any encouragement in Christ, any solace in love, any participation in the Spirit, any compassion and mercy, [2]complete my joy by being

---

"And this," he concludes, "is from God," meaning not only salvation but also the mysterious outworking of things that, on either interpretation, unbelief cannot fathom.

The next two verses (1:29-30) assert that *everything* derives from God, both the capacity "to believe"—faith is a gift (cf. Gal 3:23-25)—and "to suffer" for Christ. The Philippians share "the same struggle" which they saw in Paul when he was persecuted in Philippi (1 Thess 2:2; Acts 16:20-24) and which they now hear about as he languishes in prison. For Paul, to suffer for Christ is a privilege (Rom 5:3) and an opportunity to experience grace (2 Cor 12:8-10).

Paul's rhetoric rises to a higher pitch as he reminds the Philippians of the fundamental qualities of life "in Christ" and appeals to them to live these out in full. "If there is . . ." is purely rhetorical; there is no question of whether these qualities are present (cf. 4:8). The passage is carefully and artistically phrased, so that commentary might obscure rather than clarify. Verses 1-4 prepare for the exhortation of verse 5 and the uniquely beautiful, but also deeply theological hymn of verses 6-11. Because of its unusual wording and rhythm, some scholars believe that Paul *quotes* a hymn that he did not himself compose. In any event, he found it deeply meaningful.

The crucial phrases parallel and reinforce one another, but not merely for rhetorical effect. Paul may have in mind emerging tensions within the Philippian churches (4:2-3), which he wishes to forestall. "Encouragement in Christ" and "comfort of love" (2:1) are synonymous; "love" refers both to the love Christ has for believers and to the love he inspires in them for one another (Gal 2:20; Phil 1:9). "Participation (or 'fellowship') in the spirit" recalls Paul's blessing that has been adopted into the liturgy (2 Cor 13:13) and, more clearly than 1:27 ('in one spirit'), alludes to the Spirit of God that believers share. The words "compassion (or 'affection') and mercy" reflect Paul's insistence elsewhere on the primacy of the love-command (Rom 13:8-10; Gal 5:14).

"Complete my joy" (2:2) finishes the thought begun with all those "ifs" and recalls the great joy Paul felt with regard to the Philippians (1:4; 4:1).

of the same mind, with the same love, united in heart, thinking one thing. ³Do nothing out of selfishness or out of vainglory; rather, humbly regard others as more important than yourselves, ⁴each looking out not for his own interests, but [also] everyone for those of others.

⁵Have among yourselves the same attitude that is also yours in Christ Jesus,

---

Being "in Christ," believers can be of "the same mind" and have "the same love," that is, mutual love for one another. The next phrases—"united in heart (or 'mind'), thinking one thing"—repeat and reinforce the same notion. The words "Do nothing" (2:3) are actually not in the Greek text, though it is reasonable to supply them. Paul simply says, "Nothing out of selfishness nor from vainglory ('conceit'), but with humility regard others as more important . . ." "Others" here refers to believers; elsewhere Paul extends this love to outsiders (4:5; Gal 6:10; 1 Thess 3:12; 5:15). "Humility" and making others' interests more important than one's own (2:4, cf. 1 Cor 10:24, 33; 13:5) are not to be understood as groveling subservience; being humble has nothing to do with being a doormat (John 18:22-23). The humility Paul describes is self-sacrifice for others born out of unity in Christ. The basis for such humility is what Paul turns to in the Christ-hymn that follows.

Paul introduces the hymn with a third use of the verb *phronein* ("think") in this immediate passage (2:1-5; see 3:15); the related noun is part of the word "humility" ("lowly thinking"—2:3). It denotes an attitude or mind-set more than "thought." The New American Bible translation may be correct, but more probably Paul is simply pointing to "the attitude that is also in Christ Jesus" himself (2:5), as the opening lines of the hymn suggest. Paul presents Christ's loving and humble attitude as the model for Christian morality. The hymn itself is almost impossible to interpret in a short space; we will confine ourselves to a few essentials.

Whether the hymn is poetry as such or simply rhythmic, exalted prose, it is constructed around balanced, pregnant phrases that tell and celebrate the stages of Christ's redemptive acts for the world. It can be divided into six stanzas of three lines each, dealing with: beginning—emptying—dying—being exalted—being named—being glorified. The first half comprises Christ's actions, the second half God's. The central point is the little phrase "death on a cross." The hymn evokes and may, in some respects, be modeled on the great Servant Song of the Good Friday liturgy (Isa 52:13–53:12).

41

⁶Who, though he was in the form of God,
did not regard equality with God
something to be grasped.
⁷Rather, he emptied himself,
taking the form of a slave,
coming in human likeness;
and found human in appearance,
⁸he humbled himself,
becoming obedient to death,
even death on a cross.
⁹Because of this, God greatly exalted him
and bestowed on him the name
that is above every name,
¹⁰that at the name of Jesus
every knee should bend,
of those in heaven and on earth
and under the earth,
¹¹and every tongue confess that
Jesus Christ is Lord,
to the glory of God the Father.

Obedience and Service in the World.
¹²So then, my beloved, obedient as you have always been, not only when I am present but all the more now when I am absent, work out your salvation

The major problem of the first three lines (2:6) is whether they envisage Christ in divine preexistence ("in the form of God"), analogous to John 1:1, or as the antitype to Adam, who also was "in God's image" (Gen 1:26-27), but who, unlike Christ, "grasped at" equality with God and was disobedient (Gen 3:1-19). There are strong arguments on both sides. It is also possible—and an easy way out—that Paul might have entertained aspects of both interpretations. Other texts (notably 2 Cor 8:9; Gal 4:4; Col 1:15-17) show that the preexistence of Christ was not foreign to Paul, but Christ as the antitype of disobedient Adam is even more clearly attested (Rom 5:12-21; 1 Cor 15:22). A great deal depends on how individual phrases are translated and interpreted. "Equality with God" as "something to be *grasped at*" suggests the Adamic interpretation, but the crucial Greek word (*harpagmon*) could also be rendered "something to *be held on to*" or "*be taken advantage of.*" Overall, the Adamic interpretation is more likely, but certainty is impossible.

The next stanza ("emptying") has three phrases describing Christ's entrance into the human condition (2:7). The preexistence interpretation sees here the description of the incarnation, as in John 1:14 ("the Word became flesh") and can properly say that it was precisely in being a "slave" (not in spite of it) that Jesus revealed who God is. "Emptied himself" evokes 2 Corinthians 8:9 ("though he was rich, Christ became poor for your sake"). The Adamic view focuses on the contrast between human arrogance ("You will be like gods"—Gen 3:5) and Christ's humility.

The final stanza of the hymn's first part describes Christ's self-sacrificial death (2:7-8). All can agree that Christ's "obedience to death" is, for Paul,

with fear and trembling. ¹³For God is the one who, for his good purpose, works in you both to desire and to work. ¹⁴Do everything without grumbling or questioning, ¹⁵that you may be blameless and innocent, children of

---

the heart of the gospel, and, as here, he sometimes focuses on Jesus' death without explicit mention of the resurrection (e.g., 1 Cor 2:2; Gal 2:19-20). In the immediate context, Christ's self-emptying death provides the basis for the self-sacrifice that Paul wants the Philippians to practice toward one another (2:3-4). The nadir of the hymn is the little phrase "death on a cross," which many interpreters understand to be Paul's addition to the hymn he is quoting. That view may be correct; the phrase breaks the rhythm. On the other hand, standing at the center, it may be intended to stand alone as the turning point. Paul was not bound by rules as he either quoted or composed. However understood, it is a stark but powerful image: Christ crucified, the one on whom human redemption turns, seemingly abandoned (Mark 15:34; Gal 3:13).

"Because of this" (2:9) recalls the similar turning point in the hymn of the Suffering Servant (Isa 53:11-12) and does not primarily envisage reward for suffering but points to the *ways* of God, victory *through* suffering. God reveals in Jesus the *reversal* of human expectations by highly exalting the Crucified and bestowing on him "the name above every other name." This may refer to the exalting of the name "Jesus" itself (2:10), but probably it envisages God conferring on Jesus the name "Lord." Throughout the Old Testament, "Lord" *(kyrios)* is the translation for the sacred name YHWH, the sacred name for God (Exod 3:14; 20:7). The preexistence view of the hymn sees Jesus being raised again to his previous exalted status (cf. John 17:5). The Adamic view takes at face value that God "highly exalted" Jesus and "gave him a name" he did not previously have (cf. Acts 2:36; Rom 1:3-4). The latter view is not, of course, a denial of Jesus' divine nature but simply says that it was *not yet so fully* articulated. That Paul saw Jesus as "the Son of God" is quite clear (e.g., Rom 8:2, 32; Gal 4:4), but in Paul's time the formulations of the Nicene Creed were far in the future.

Be that as it may, the present text provides clear precedent for later formulations. Isaiah 45:23, clearly quoted in 2:10-11 ("every knee shall bend . . . every tongue confess") applies to Jesus words that the text from Isaiah uses of God; all creation and all parts of creation will own and confess that "Jesus is Lord" (Rom 10:9; 1 Cor 12:3) and in glorifying Jesus will glorify "God the Father." So concludes this remarkable hymn. Its second half is

God without blemish in the midst of a crooked and perverse generation, among whom you shine like lights in the world, ¹⁶as you hold on to the word of life, so that my boast for the day of Christ may be that I did not run in vain or labor in vain. ¹⁷But, even if I am poured out as a libation upon the sacrificial service of your faith, I rejoice and share my joy with all of you. ¹⁸In the same way you also should rejoice and share your joy with me.

not as relevant to Paul's point that believers are to imitate the humility of Jesus. Nevertheless, in depicting also the final stage of Christ's self-sacrifice, it enables believers to have a greater vision of the path of faith.

In the next paragraph (2:12-18) Paul uses the example of Christ to exhort the Philippians to both greater effort and a deeper vision. Of great interest is the command "Work out your own salvation." It arises from mention of Paul's "absence." When present, *he* worked for their salvation; now "all the more" he throws the responsibility on them. It is a remarkable command, however, because usually salvation, for Paul, is exclusively *God's* work (e.g., 1 Thess 5:9) and, in fact, he hastens to correct any misunderstanding by emphasizing that "*God* is the one who . . . works in you both to desire and to work" for salvation (2:13; cf. 1:29). Nevertheless, Paul also knows that humans have a part in the salvation of themselves and of those close to them (Rom 11:14; 1 Cor 7:16; 9:22); believers' conduct does matter.

The difference, therefore, between believers and the world ought to be apparent. Believers "shine like stars in the cosmos" (2:15), but not if "quarrels and disputes" (2:14) mark their behavior. The world, says Paul, is "crooked and perverse"; believers are to be "innocent." This can come across as an idyllic, unrealistic vision, but Paul presupposes a community where *every* member "works for salvation." There is here no handing over of responsibility to a class of "ministers and overseers" (1:1); all together "hold on to the word of life" and will prove the value of Paul's "labor" on "the day of Christ" (2:16). Meanwhile, for all his apparent optimism (1:25; 2:24), Paul acknowledges that he may be "poured out as a libation," almost certainly a reference to martyrdom (2 Tim 4:6). "Sacrifice and service" is the language of temple worship and is used elsewhere both of Paul (Rom 15:16) and of believers generally (Rom 12:1; 15:27; Phil 2:30; 4:18). Paul would find death a reason for "rejoicing" (1:23; cf. 3:10), and if it happens, he asks that the Philippians "rejoice with" him (2:18)!

IV. Travel Plans of Paul
and His Assistants

Timothy and Paul. ¹⁹I hope, in the Lord Jesus, to send Timothy to you soon, so that I too may be heartened by hearing news of you. ²⁰For I have no one comparable to him for genuine interest in whatever concerns you. ²¹For they all seek their own interests, not those of Jesus Christ. ²²But you know his worth, how as a child with a father he served along with me in the cause of the gospel. ²³He it is, then, whom I hope to send as soon as I see how things go with me, ²⁴but I am confident in the Lord that I myself will also come soon.

Epaphroditus. ²⁵With regard to Epaphroditus, my brother and co-worker

---

2:19–3:1 Travel plans

Paul often includes, usually toward the end of his letters (see Rom 15:14-32; 1 Cor 16:5-12), some indication of the travel plans for himself and others. He hopes "to send Timothy soon" (2:19) so that he will be able to bring back good news. Paul takes this occasion to speak very warmly of Timothy (1:1; Acts 16:1), who was like a devoted child to the apostle (1:22). Paul also hopes that he himself will soon be able to come to Philippi (1:24).

He thinks it even more urgent "to send Epaphroditus," who came as "an apostle" of the Philippians (2:25), bearing their gift (4:18). The next verses suggest regular communications between Paul in prison and the Philippians. They have heard that Epaphroditus fell seriously ill ("close to death"—2:27, 30), and word has come back of their concern, so that now Epaphroditus is concerned for *them* (2:26, 28). Though he figures nowhere else in the New Testament, he was a "co-worker" with Paul for a while (2:25). Paul regarded it as a mercy of God that Epaphroditus recovered from his illness (2:27) and is concerned that the Philippians should receive him warmly and "hold such people in high regard" (2:29; cf. 1 Thess 5:13). He "risked his life" both "for the work of Christ" and for the "service" the Philippians wished to render to Paul (2:30).

The word "finally" (3:1) can signal the near conclusion of a letter (2 Cor 13:11; cf. Eph 6:10; 2 Thess 3:1) or the conclusion of one topic and transition to another (1 Cor 7:29; 1 Thess 4:1). Here, following "travel plans," the letter should be drawing to a close, but it does not, and it is unusual that there is a second "finally" (4:8). Further, the natural sequence of "Rejoice in the Lord" (3:1) is either 4:1 or 4:4, certainly not 3:2! These observations have convinced scholars either that Philippians comprises more than one letter (the majority view) or that something has caused Paul to create a very awkward transition after 3:1. In any event, 3:1 or at

and fellow soldier, your messenger and minister in my need, I consider it necessary to send him to you. [26]For he has been longing for all of you and was distressed because you heard that he was ill. [27]He was indeed ill, close to death; but God had mercy on him, not just on him but also on me, so that I might not have sorrow upon sorrow. [28]I send him therefore with the greater eagerness, so that, on seeing him, you may rejoice again, and I may have less anxiety. [29]Welcome him then in the Lord with all joy and hold such people in esteem, [30]because for the sake of the work of Christ he came close to death, risking his life to make up for those services to me that you could not perform.

3 **Concluding Admonitions.** [1]Finally, my brothers, rejoice in the Lord.

Writing the same things to you is no burden for me but is a safeguard for you.

V. Polemic: Righteousness and the Goal in Christ

Against Legalistic Teachers. [2]Beware of the dogs! Beware of the evil-workers! Beware of the mutilation! [3]For we are the circumcision, we who worship through the Spirit of God, who boast in Christ Jesus and do not put our confidence in flesh, [4]although I myself have grounds for confidence even in the flesh.

Paul's Autobiography. If anyone else thinks he can be confident in flesh, all the more can I. [5]Circumcised on the eighth day, of the race of Israel, of the tribe of Benjamin, a Hebrew of Hebrew

least the command to "rejoice in the Lord" concludes the first (half of the) letter, recalling one of its major themes. It is "no burden" to him to repeat himself (about joy), but it is rather a "safeguard" for them (cf. Neh 8:10; Pss 81:1; 21.1).

3:2-11 An urgent warning against false faith

This paragraph shows how Paul's feelings of affection can burst into anger at those who would threaten the direction of believers' faith in Christ. The threat probably comes from conservative Jewish Christians, similar to those he contended with in Galatians. In that case the opponents were already present (Gal 1:6-7; 6:12). In this case Paul seems simply to be afraid of their imminent arrival in Philippi, and he uses harsh invectives to emphasize that such persons are not to be trusted. In calling them "dogs," he turns on them a common Jewish epithet directed at Gentiles (Mark 7:27); "evildoers" may be an ironic twist on their claim to be "law-doers," and "mutilation" *(katatome)* is a sarcastic reference to their insistence on "circumcision" *(peritome*—3:2; cf. Gal 6:12). *They* are not the true "circumcision," says Paul; *"we are,"* we "who worship through the Spirit of God" (3:3).

parentage, in observance of the law a Pharisee, ⁶in zeal I persecuted the church, in righteousness based on the law I was blameless.

Righteousness from God. ⁷[But] whatever gains I had, these I have come to consider a loss because of Christ. ⁸More than that, I even consider everything as a loss because of the supreme good of knowing Christ Jesus my Lord. For his sake I have accepted the loss of all things and I consider them so much

---

The opponents claim that with their adherence to the traditions and laws of Israel, *they* represent the true "Israel" ("descendants of Abraham" —Gal 3:6-9, 29). Paul insists that they are nothing of the kind and sees this as an urgent issue, because it has to do with whether believers have "confidence" in Christ—note the repetition of this word (3:3-4)—or implicitly regard Christ's death as worthless (cf. Gal 2:20-21). By his conversion Paul was convinced that the covenant, from Abraham on, was founded simply on grace and faith (Rom 4:1-5; 9:6-16); the law was secondary (Rom 4:13-17; Gal 3:15-17).

Paul's critique of these Jewish-Christian opponents must *not* be taken as a critique of Judaism, as has too often been the case. Paul's love of his heritage (e.g., Rom 9:1-5) and his confidence that God would be faithful to the covenant with them (Rom 11:1-2, 29) are well attested. The enduring value of God's covenant with the Jews was also strongly affirmed at the Second Vatican Council. This polemic has to do with particular circumstances in Philippi, not with Judaism as such.

Paul presents himself as the model to follow. If circumcision or law-obedience were crucial, Paul would have "even more" reason for "confidence" than the opponents (3:4). There follows in verses 5-6 his recounting of the privileges he enjoyed by birth and his chosen way of life as a "Pharisee," all of which attest to his unique pedigree as a devoted member of the chosen people. His "zeal" for the law, in which he had been "blameless" (3:6), had even extended to persecution of the church (cf. 1 Cor 15:9; Gal 1:13-14; Acts 7:58–8:3; 9:1-2). But what he had once thought of as "gains," now "because of Christ" he reckons as "loss" (3:7). No human privilege or achievement "counts" for anything when compared with "the supreme good of knowing Christ Jesus my Lord" (3:8).

The key issue for Paul in all his letters is the nature of the divine-human relationship—specifically, by what is it characterized? As here, he rejects law and tradition as its foundation; elsewhere he rejects human wisdom or any kind of superior status, whether religious or social (Rom 2:17-29; 1 Cor 1:18-31). All such "gains" are simply "so much rubbish";

rubbish, that I may gain Christ [9]and be found in him, not having any righteousness of my own based on the law but that which comes through faith in Christ, the righteousness from God, depending on faith [10]to know him and the power of his resurrection and [the] sharing of his sufferings by being conformed to his death, [11]if somehow I may attain the resurrection from the dead.

Forward in Christ. [12]It is not that I have already taken hold of it or have already attained perfect maturity, but I continue my pursuit in hope that I may possess it, since I have indeed been taken possession of by Christ [Jesus]. [13]Brothers, I for my part do not consider myself to have taken possession. Just one thing: forgetting what lies behind but straining forward to what lies ahead, [14]I continue my pursuit toward the

what matters is to "know Christ" (3:8), which means to have "faith in" him (3:9), in the sense of joyful trust. To "be found in him" looks forward to the judgment, when those who are "in Christ" will have no reason for fear (2:16).

Verses 9-11 describe the purpose of letting go of former privileges and status: it is "to know him and the power of his resurrection" (3:10). "Resurrection," however, is not merely in the future; it is a *present* experience, even in the midst of suffering (2 Cor 4:7-18; 5:17). To be "in Christ" is already to "walk in newness of life" (Rom 6:4; cf. 7:6). None of this, however, is a human accomplishment. The relationship ("righteousness") believers enjoy with God derives from a "righteousness" gained by Christ that is conferred as a gift; it is not essentially dependent on law or tradition (3:9). Even "faith" (3:9) is not the *condition* of "righteousness" but simply the *way it is lived*.

3:12-21 The ongoing journey toward Christ

Having stressed again *God's* initiative (cf. 1:29; 2:13), Paul turns emphatically to the theme of human responsibility, though even here Christ's action is prominent. He uses a series of verbs ("received," "made perfect," "pursue") to describe the *process* of "straining forward" toward "perfection" in Christ. He is at pains to say that, to be sure, he is not totally "perfected," but that, as he wishes them to do, he makes maximum effort to "possess" that for which he is already "possessed by Christ" (3:12). Therefore, he lets go of "the past" and sets his sights only on "the prize of God's upward calling" (3:13-14). Paul may again have death in mind (cf. 1:23; 2:17), but "calling" is an important word in his letters to denote both the event of conversion and the life of faith to which it leads (e.g., Rom 4:17; 8:30; 1 Cor 1:9, 26; 7:15-24). Paul considers himself and others as, in a

goal, the prize of God's upward calling, in Christ Jesus. [15]Let us, then, who are "perfectly mature" adopt this attitude. And if you have a different attitude, this too God will reveal to you. [16]Only, with regard to what we have attained, continue on the same course.

Wrong Conduct and Our Goal. [17]Join with others in being imitators of me, brothers, and observe those who thus conduct themselves according to the model you have in us. [18]For many, as I have often told you and now tell you even in tears, conduct themselves as enemies of the cross of Christ. [19]Their end is destruction. Their God is their stomach; their glory is in their "shame." Their minds are occupied with earthly things. [20]But our citizenship is in heaven, and from it we also await a

sense, "perfect" (3:15, cf. 1 Cor 2:6; Matt 5:48), but this perfection consists in the "attitude," which he wants the Philippians to have, of *striving* for perfection! If some are inclined to disagree (cf. 1 Cor 11:16), Paul is sure that he is right and that "God will reveal this also" to them. Meanwhile they should remain constant in the progress already attained (3:16) and join together in being "imitators" of Paul and of those whose behavior is a true model.

Paul's confidence in himself, that he is a proper guide and "model" for believers, should not be seen as arrogance. The ultimate example he has in mind is Christ in his self-emptying death (2:6-8), to which all believers are to seek to be "conformed" (3:10). Paul's self-assurance derives from long years of having lived in imitation of the self-sacrificial example of Jesus. On the other hand, "there are many" whose behavior makes them "the enemies of the cross" (3:18). Paul had "often" told the Philippians of such people; they, therefore, must have known who they were. We, however, can only plead ignorance. Perhaps they are the opponents Paul inveighs against in 3:2, but that is not clear. The criticisms of them are very vague, but they may indicate moral laxity of some kind. A warning against laxity also appears in Galatians (Gal 5:13-26) following that letter's stern teaching against being overly concerned with law. The pattern here is similar.

By contrast with such people, whose "minds are set on earthly things" (3:19), "*our* citizenship is in heaven, from where we await a *savior*, the Lord." "Citizenship" (cf. 1:27) and "savior" are never found again in Paul's own letters; they are suited very specifically for this city with its "Roman" citizenry, which acknowledged the *emperor* (probably Nero) as "Lord" and "Savior." The contrasting of the emperor with Jesus is undoubtedly deliberate, though Paul is not preaching political rebellion (cf. Rom 13:1-7). His point is precisely that believers' hope is *not* in politics. Believers'

savior, the Lord Jesus Christ. [21]He will change our lowly body to conform with his glorified body by the power that enables him also to bring all things into subjection to himself.

VI. Instructions for the Community

4 **Live in Concord.** [1]Therefore, my brothers, whom I love and long for, my joy and crown, in this way stand firm in the Lord, beloved.

[2]I urge Euodia and I urge Syntyche to come to a mutual understanding in the Lord. [3]Yes, and I ask you also, my true yokemate, to help them, for they have struggled at my side in promoting the gospel, along with Clement and my other co-workers, whose names are in the book of life.

Joy and Peace. [4]Rejoice in the Lord always. I shall say it again: rejoice! [5]Your kindness should be known to all.

---

hope is in Christ, who will, at his coming, "change our lowly body to conform with his glorified body" (3:21), a theme that Paul develops at length elsewhere (1 Cor 15:35-57). The *present* experience of *gradually* "being transformed" into the image of the Lord (2 Cor 3:18) anticipates that future "change" at the resurrection. Gradual transformation is what Paul has largely had in mind since 3:10.

4:1-9 Final appeals and exhortations

The opening demonstrates once again Paul's deep affection for, and joy in, the Philippians. We never hear elsewhere of Euodia and Syntyche. The appeal to them to "have the same mind" is the same plea of 2:2 (Rom 15:5). Paul asks his "true yokemate" (*Syzygos*—perhaps a proper name) to "assist them," probably meaning to act as an arbitrator. They were important leaders of the church in Philippi, having been foundational, along with Lydia (Acts 16:13-15), in establishing the church there. We cannot know what their dispute was, and in any case it was not overly serious; Paul has confidence that they will work it out. We also do not know anything more about "Syzygos." The word (name?) is masculine; this is not a reference, as is sometimes supposed, to Paul's wife.

Paul exhorts them all yet again to "rejoice." In that joy their "kindness" (or "gentleness") can and should "be known to all" (4:5). "The Lord is near" refers to the soon-expected "day of Christ" (2:16; cf. 3:20). In the meantime they must not "worry"; that would be the opposite of joy. They must simply make their prayers and requests known to God (4:6), and "the peace of God" (cf. John 14:27), which has to do with far more than the absence of conflict or suffering (1:29), "will guard their hearts and minds" (4:7). "Peace" is the gift that flows from "grace" (1:2; Rom 5:1-11). "Finally" Paul exhorts them simply to hold fast to all that is good and repeats

The Lord is near. ⁶Have no anxiety at all, but in everything, by prayer and petition, with thanksgiving, make your requests known to God. ⁷Then the peace of God that surpasses all understanding will guard your hearts and minds in Christ Jesus.

⁸Finally, brothers, whatever is true, whatever is honorable, whatever is just, whatever is pure, whatever is lovely, whatever is gracious, if there is any excellence and if there is anything worthy of praise, think about these things. ⁹Keep on doing what you have learned and received and heard and seen in me. Then the God of peace will be with you.

VII. Gratitude for the Philippians' Generosity

¹⁰I rejoice greatly in the Lord that now at last you revived your concern for me. You were, of course, concerned about me but lacked an opportunity. ¹¹Not that I say this because of need, for I have learned, in whatever situation I find myself, to be self-sufficient. ¹²I know indeed how to live in humble circumstances; I know also how to live with abundance. In every circumstance and in all things I have learned the secret of being well fed and of going hungry, of living in abundance and of being in need. ¹³I have the strength for

again the theme of learning from and imitating his manner of following Christ. The "peace" blessing is also found elsewhere (Rom 15:33; 2 Cor 13:11).

4:10-20 Thanks for the Philippians' generosity

Many commentators regard this section as "letter A," sent before the other letter(s) as a thank-you note. That could be correct, but this is not the first time Paul has received a gift from the Philippians (4:16; cf. 2 Cor 11:9); this is the "revival" of their generosity—not that their concern had flagged, but they "lacked the opportunity" to show it (4:10). Now, however, Epaphroditus has delivered their gift (4:18), and Paul rejoices at their concern and, as is typical, not only gives thanks for the material blessing but also reflects on the spiritual riches he has in Christ (4:13). As elsewhere, Paul can appear slightly arrogant as he assures them that he has "learned" to be "self-sufficient" (4:11-12). He just barely says "thanks" (4:14), but his tone is not so much arrogant as embarrassed.

Elsewhere, especially in the Corinthian letters (1 Cor 9:3-18; 2 Cor 12:13-16), Paul refused to exercise his "right" to be paid for his apostolic work, "working night and day" rather than be a burden on anyone (1 Thess 2:9). For some reason, however, he had long ago entered into a financial arrangement with the Philippians (4:15) but was hesitant to accept their money. It might appear that he wanted their *possessions* rather than *themselves* (2 Cor 12:14) and be no better than other "peddlers of the

everything through him who empowers me. [14]Still, it was kind of you to share in my distress.

[15]You Philippians indeed know that at the beginning of the gospel, when I left Macedonia, not a single church shared with me in an account of giving and receiving, except you alone. [16]For even when I was at Thessalonica you sent me something for my needs, not only once but more than once. [17]It is not that I am eager for the gift; rather, I am eager for the profit that accrues to your account. [18]I have received full payment and I abound. I am very well supplied because of what I received from you through Epaphroditus, "a fragrant aroma," an acceptable sacrifice, pleasing to God. [19]My God will fully supply whatever you need, in accord with his glorious riches in Christ Jesus. [20]To our God and Father, glory forever and ever. Amen.

VIII. Farewell

[21]Give my greetings to every holy one in Christ Jesus. The brothers who are with me send you their greetings; [22]all the holy ones send you their greetings, especially those of Caesar's household. [23]The grace of the Lord Jesus Christ be with your spirit.

---

word of God" (2 Cor 2:17). Further, his enemies might say that he appropriated for himself (2 Cor 8:20-21) money he had promised to collect for Jerusalem (Gal 2:10; Rom 15:25-26). So he assures the Philippians that he is "not eager for the gift" but for "the profit that accrues to *their* account" (4:17). The money is fully adequate to his needs, but, more important, it is "an acceptable sacrifice, pleasing to God" (4:18). And God will also fill their every need "according to his wealth in glory" (4:19). Paul concludes his thank-you in the manner of a prayer, giving glory to God (4:20).

4:21-23 Final greetings and blessing

The sending of greetings is common enough (see 1 Cor 16:19-20; 2 Cor 13:12), but particular here is the mention of greetings from some in "Caesar's household" (4:22), which to many suggests that Paul was in Rome. This is possible, but Caesar's officials and servants were in major cities throughout the empire, including Philippi. The mention of Caesar (only here in Paul's letters; cf. Rom 13:1-7) would be meaningful for this Roman colony. Paul ends the letter with his standard blessing (1 Cor 16:23; Gal 6:18); it echoes his opening greeting (1:2). "Grace" is the beginning and end of Christian existence.

The Second Letter to the Thessalonians

The challenges of 2 Thessalonians

For being such a short letter, 2 Thessalonians presents a surprising number of challenges for modern interpreters. A primary issue is whether or not the letter was written by Paul himself, with most scholars these days believing that it was not. A second major issue is the letter's situation: when was it written, who were its intended recipients, what were their problems, and where were they located? Those problems are difficult enough and also have to be answered for a few other New Testament books, but they pale in comparison with the difficulty of understanding what the author says in the central part of the letter. What is meant by "the restrainer" in 2:6-7? Is this a good or an evil power? In fact, is "restrainer" even the correct translation of the Greek term? And who is "the rebel" (or "the lawless one") in 2:3-9, whose coming "springs from the power of Satan"? These problems of 2:3-9 will be dealt with in the commentary itself; the other problems need to be clarified, as far as possible, immediately.

Who wrote 2 Thessalonians?

There are several New Testament letters which the ancient church accepted as written by Paul but which modern scholarship, for good reasons, believes he did not write. Almost all scholars have long regarded the Pastoral Epistles (1 and 2 Timothy and Titus) as not written by Paul; Ephesians, Colossians, and 2 Thessalonians comprise a middle group, whose authenticity has been doubted. Complete certainty is impossible, but in recent years *most*, though not all, scholars have come to accept that 2 Thessalonians was not written by Paul.

Although, superficially, the letter appears to be authentic, closer examination shows that it uses Paul's style and vocabulary in a strange way. It

53

imitates and even, at points, copies from the earlier letter, using it as a model. For example, 2 Thessalonians 1:1 repeats the opening of 1 Thessalonians almost word for word, a practice otherwise unknown among Paul's letters. Even 2 Corinthians 1:1-2, initially almost identical to 1 Corinthians 1:1-3, ultimately differs substantially. The second letter (2 Thess 2:13) has a second thanksgiving, imitating a unique feature of 1 Thessalonians, and the prayers in 2:16 and 3:16 appear to be modeled on prayers in the earlier letter (1 Thess 3:11; 5:23). Furthermore, 2 Thessalonians 3:8 largely repeats 1 Thessalonians 2:9. Such similarities might ordinarily be expected to indicate the same author, but actually copying and imitating his own writing is not a feature of Paul's certainly authentic letters.

In addition to such unexpected imitation, there are also some unexpected stylistic differences. In 2 Thessalonians there is a strange predominance of long, complex sentences (e.g., 2 Thess 1:3-10—one sentence in Greek!) and of long noun-phrases (e.g., 2:8-10). To be sure, such features also appear in the certainly authentic letters, but not to this extent. In a detailed examination of such stylistic peculiarities, one author has shown that 2 Thessalonians resembles Colossians and Ephesians, whose authenticity is also doubted.

In addition to these stylistic observations, the theology of 2 Thessalonians does not appear authentic; most notably, its central section (2:1-12) clashes strangely with Paul's eschatological teaching in 1 Thessalonians 4–5. The latter presupposes that the end is very close (e.g., 4:15, "we who are *alive,* who *remain* at the coming of the Lord") but envisages no way to calculate the time of the end (5:1-3). This is consistent with Paul's views elsewhere (e.g., Rom 13:11-12; 1 Cor 7:29) and with Mark 13:32 ("About that day or hour no one knows, not the angels in heaven nor even the Son"). However, 2 Thessalonians 2:1-6 presupposes that such calculation is possible and even claims that Paul had instructed the readers about it (2:5).

Furthermore, for being such a short letter, 2 Thessalonians has an unusual number of appeals to the letters and tradition of Paul and his companions (2:2, 15; 3:6, 14, 17) and an unusual number of reminders of when Paul was with them (2:5; 3:10, cf. 2:14). The impression is that the writer of 2 Thessalonians had to go to unusual lengths to "authenticate" this letter as being from "Paul." This is consistent with the situation at the end of the first century, twenty to thirty years after Paul's death, when the apostle had become a revered figure and it was important to appeal to his authority to settle difficult questions.

The Arch of Galerius in Thessalonica, erected in A.D. *304 to commemorate victories over the Persians*

In this regard, one author has noted that Paul himself, when giving information about "the end," did so not only on his own authority but also by appeal to "a mystery" or "a word of the Lord" (note 1 Cor 15:51; 1 Thess 4:15), which is in line with apocalyptic writing in general (e.g., Dan 7:15-16; Rev 1:2; 22:16). In 2 Thessalonians 2:3-12, however, the only source is "Paul" himself. For this writer, Paul has become the higher authority, and thus a letter in his name will suffice to settle the present crisis about an apocalyptic question.

Further, though pretending to derive from Paul, 2 Thessalonians is unusually lacking in expressions of love. In the authentic letters Paul is effusively affectionate (e.g., Phil 1:8; 2:12; 4:1), and, in fact, nowhere is this more evident than in 1 Thessalonians (e.g., 1 Thess 2:7-8, 17). Even when angry, Paul expresses affection (1 Cor 4:14-15; 10:14; 2 Cor 11:11; Gal 4:19-20). That Paul would write to the Thessalonians at a time when they were suffering greatly and would not express personal affection is unthinkable.

In modern culture, to write a text and place someone else's name on it comes across as fraudulent, but in the ancient Greco-Roman world it was not so unusual, and, in fact, the character of Paul's ministry makes such letters unsurprising. First, like many others, Paul *dictated* his letters to secretaries, people like Tertius (Rom 16:22, "I, Tertius, who wrote this letter greet you in the Lord"). Such secretaries could sometimes have an influence on the way things were expressed.

Second, and more important, Paul included others, named and unnamed (1 Thess 1:1, "Timothy, Silvanus"; Gal 1:2, "all the believers with me"), among the senders of his letters, though he himself seems to have been the only real author in most cases. This reflects the collaborative nature of Paul's missionary endeavors. Therefore, just as it was natural for Paul to write in their names, so it was natural, when Paul was not around, for them to write in his name, even after his death.

And third, both Jewish and Greco-Roman societies knew of many examples of texts being written in the name of famous dead people (e.g., Psalms of Solomon, Letters of Plato). As in many of those cases, so in the case of Paul's co-workers and successors, the purpose was not fraud for profit, but simply to appeal to the apostle's authority to help those who stood in the tradition of his teaching.

It is, of course, impossible to prove in any definitive way whether or not Paul wrote this letter. People of good faith can reasonably disagree on this matter, as is also the case with other disputed books. Modern believers properly focus, not on such historical questions, but on the theology and spirituality of the texts. However, in our attempts to understand Paul, it is perhaps important to realize that not everything that goes under his name necessarily conveys an accurate portrait of him and his theology.

The situation of the letter

Who, then, did write 2 Thessalonians and, more important, when and under what circumstances? Evidently the letter intends to guide believers "about the coming of our Lord Jesus" (2:1) in the context of persecution (1:4) and particularly to warn them against those who claim that "the day of the Lord is [already] here" (2:2). After the destruction of Jerusalem by the Romans (A.D. 70), confusion and speculation about the time of the end were rife (e.g., Mark 13:5-7; 2 Pet 3:3-10). The book of Revelation suggests (e.g., 13:7) that in the nineties (under the emperor Domitian) persecution of believers in Asia Minor was a major problem. Many scholars think that this may be the context also of 2 Thessalonians. If so, then the letter was written to a real situation, but not to a specific community. It is meant to remind believers in various churches (see Rev 2–3) of established apostolic tradition (2:15) so that they are not "shaken out of [their] minds" by the claims of more recent teachers (2:2).

This need to appeal to authoritative tradition explains why the author used 1 Thessalonians as a model and insisted that what he wrote truly came from the apostle's hand (2 Thess 3:17). Such appeals to older authority are found elsewhere in Scripture (e.g., Daniel, Pastoral Epistles).

Interpreting 2 Thessalonians in the church today

The debate about authorship and the uncertainties of it remind us to be humble in the face of questions we cannot definitively settle and to maintain a careful balance in interpreting Scripture. Reason, as well as faith, is a gift of God, and reason, along with tradition and doctrine, is to guide interpretation of the Bible. Regardless of authorship, 2 Thessalonians is sacred Scripture that can still speak to the heart of the church.

"Literal" interpretations, which imagine that biblical texts were written with the early twenty-first century in mind, only introduce the sorts of confusions that 2 Thessalonians warns against. A true "literal" interpretation never forgets the letter's first-century context and what the author wanted to accomplish in that time among those believers. It also does not forget the limited perspective and knowledge of the ancient writer, who, like Paul himself, expected the end to come very soon. It is not a disparagement of the ancient texts when we admit that such expectations were mistaken. The texts have remained valuable in every generation for their spiritual wisdom and their witness to the faith-experience of first-century believers; their value does not reside either in exact recall of historical events or in precise delineations of God's future plans. The Scriptures, though inspired, have their limitations, just as we, in the midst of our limitations, are not without divine inspiration.

The church today is not, for the most part, persecuted, as was the church to which this letter was addressed. But the church today has its own sufferings and perplexities and can gain much from contemplating the courage and perseverance of ancient believers. We cannot identify with everything this letter has to say, but if we look carefully beneath the surface, we can discover that the same divine Spirit that urged and consoled believers then is still with us in the modern world.

The Second Letter to the Thessalonians

I. Address

1 **Greeting.** [1]Paul, Silvanus, and Timothy to the church of the Thessalonians in God our Father and the Lord Jesus Christ: [2]grace to you and peace from God [our] Father and the Lord Jesus Christ.

Thanksgiving. [3]We ought to thank God always for you, brothers, as is fitting, because your faith flourishes ever more, and the love of every one of you for one another grows ever greater. [4]Accordingly, we ourselves boast of you in the churches of God regarding your endurance and faith in all your persecutions and the afflictions you endure.

[5]This is evidence of the just judgment of God, so that you may be considered worthy of the kingdom of God

1:1-2 Prescript and greeting

The prescript (1:1), which, in accordance with ancient style, includes the sender's and recipient's names, is an exact copy of 1 Thessalonians 1:1, adding only the word "our." If Paul is not the real author, it is *possible* that either Silvanus or Timothy might be. The greeting (1:2) is identical to the longer greeting of Paul's authentic letters and, in that regard, differs slightly from 1 Thessalonians. This may indicate that the author knew the other letters; the model for this one, however, is certainly 1 Thessalonians. "Grace and peace" (2:16; 3:16) were primary theological terms, being respectively the foundation and the fruit of the gospel (e.g., Rom 5:1-2).

1:3-12 The (first) thanksgiving

Proportional to the length of the letter, this is an amazingly long thanksgiving (cf. Rom 1:8-15), and, even more remarkable, 1:3-10 comprises in Greek one long, very complex sentence. This is one of the reasons for thinking that Paul did not write it. Nevertheless, it contains a number of challenging ideas, which in part reflect 1 Thessalonians and in part are somewhat unique. "We *ought* to give thanks" (also 2:13) is awkward phrasing, never used by Paul himself, but the reasons for thanks are very much in Paul's tradition, in that fidelity to the gospel (Phil 1:5) and the fruitfulness of God's gifts among believers (1 Cor 1:4) were always important

for which you are suffering. ⁶For it is surely just on God's part to repay with afflictions those who are afflicting you, ⁷and to grant rest along with us to you who are undergoing afflictions, at the revelation of the Lord Jesus from heaven with his mighty angels, ⁸in blazing fire, inflicting punishment on those who do not acknowledge God and on those who do not obey the gospel of our Lord Jesus. ⁹These will pay the penalty of eternal ruin, separated from the presence of the Lord and from the glory of his power, ¹⁰when he comes to be glorified among his holy ones and to be marveled at on that day among all who have believed, for our testimony to you was believed. ▶

for the apostle. In this case the writer especially commends believers for their growth in faith and love, even in the midst of "persecutions and afflictions." The themes of faith and love (1:3), of the Thessalonians as model believers (1:4), and of looking forward to Christ's coming judgment (1:7, 9) are all reminiscent of the initial thanksgiving in 1 Thessalonians and were important ideas for Paul himself.

Not typical of Paul is the lengthy dwelling here on the theme of divine retribution for "those who are afflicting you" (1:6). Presumably the latter are identical with those who "do not acknowledge God and do not obey the gospel" (1:8), though it is possible the writer has different groups in mind. The idea of severe retribution appears again in 2:10-12, making this letter far harsher and more vengeful in its tone than any other letter under Paul's name. Such passages are usually, and understandably, not popular, and care is indeed needed in their interpretation.

Harsh, condemnatory warnings, however, are found throughout Scripture, including sayings from Jesus (e.g., Luke 13:1-9); they are not confined, as is sometimes imagined, to the Old Testament. They express God's rejection of evil and bias for justice, but also the human authors' anger, especially in the face of persecution. They are, it must be emphasized, more than outweighed by expressions of God's love and mercy (e.g., Exod 34:6-7; Luke 15:11-32) and by the demand that believers must love their enemies (e.g., Lev 19:33-34; Matt 5:31-38). The harshness of this letter undoubtedly reflects the bitter experience of religious persecution.

The consolation for believers is that God's judgment is just (1:5), as is shown in their being "considered worthy of the kingdom of God" for which they suffer (cf. 1:11, praying "that our God make you worthy of the

▶ This symbol indicates a cross reference number in the *Catechism of the Catholic Church.* See page 123 for number citations.

Prayer. [11]To this end, we always pray for you, that our God may make you worthy of his calling and powerfully bring to fulfillment every good purpose and every effort of faith, [12]that the name of our Lord Jesus may be glorified in you, and you in him, in accord with the grace of our God and Lord Jesus Christ.

II. Warning Against Deception Concerning the Parousia

Christ and the Lawless One. [1]We ask you, brothers, with regard to

---

call"). Behind this is the idea, important for Paul himself, that salvation derives "not from human desiring or striving, but from God who has mercy" (Rom 9:16; cf. Eph 2:8-9). "The revelation of the Lord Jesus from heaven with his mighty angels" (1:7) recalls 1 Thessalonians 3:13 and various other apocalyptic texts (e.g., Matt 24:31). Also typical of apocalypticism is the expectation of "blazing fire" at the end (e.g., 1 Cor 3:13-15; Isa 66:15-16), delivering punishment for the "disobedient," who will be "separated from the presence of the Lord." On the other hand, "on that day" of judgment the Lord will "be glorified among his holy ones" and "be marveled at by all who have believed" (1:10).

The writer personalizes this general description by saying that the reason for the "glorifying" and "marveling" was that "our testimony to *you* was believed" (1:10); believers will be a cause for celebration on judgment day. "Holy ones" here, as in 1 Thessalonians 3:13, probably refers to "his mighty angels" who will accompany him (1:7), so that the writer envisages the earthly believers joining the heavenly host in triumphant praise of the Lord (see Phil 2:10-11; Rev 7:9-17).

The thanksgiving concludes with a prayer that is somewhat reminiscent of 1 Thessalonians 1:2-3. The prayer asks that God "might make believers worthy" and "complete" their "every good purpose and work of faith." The latter phrase is also found in 1 Thessalonians 1:3 but otherwise is slightly unusual for Paul (cf. Rom 3:27-28; 9:32).

2:1-12 The central problem: Is this the end of the world?

After that long thanksgiving, finally the heart of the matter: "the coming *(parousia)* of our Lord Jesus Christ and our being gathered to him" (not "with him"). The readers have been radically "shaken out of [their] minds" by the claim that "the day of the Lord is here" (not merely "at hand"). The writer does not know whether it is some spirit-filled utterance that has disturbed them or a "word" of prophecy or even a "letter" claiming to be from Paul. Whatever it is, it is deceitful. This imprecision,

the coming of our Lord Jesus Christ and our assembling with him, ²not to be shaken out of your minds suddenly, or to be alarmed either by a "spirit," or by an oral statement, or by a letter allegedly from us to the effect that the day of the Lord is at hand. ³Let no one deceive you in any way. For unless the apostasy comes first and the lawless one is revealed, the one doomed to perdition, ⁴who opposes and exalts himself above every so-called god and object of worship, so as to seat himself in the temple of God, claiming that he is a god—⁵do you not recall that while I was still with you I told you these things? ⁶And now you know what is restraining, that he may be revealed in his time. ⁷For the mystery of lawlessness is already at work. But the one

with the writer covering all bases, suggests that the letter is not written to a specific, known situation but is intended to respond to some end-of-the-century situation(s) in which persecutions had convinced believers that history was all but over.

Verse 2 provides glimpses into early church worship that enable us to see how ecstatic speech and prophecies, while deeply valued, also had to be regulated and subjected to discernment (cf. 1 Cor 14:29-32). First Thessalonians 5:19-21 also advises, "Do not extinguish the spirit, do not despise prophecies, but *test everything*"! The human condition is such that "spirit" and prophecy are inevitably ambiguous; not everything that claims to be from God necessarily is so. The readers are envisioned as profoundly shaken by some communication, possibly even "a letter pretending to be from Paul," that has them convinced that the end of the world is already here! In 3:11 it appears that some have even ceased working because of this conviction.

The writer urges the Thessalonians not to be deceived "in any way" and then begins an explanation (vv. 3-8) of why they should realize that "the day of the Lord" has not yet come (cf. Mark 13:5-7, "Beware, lest anyone deceive you . . . the end is not yet!"). This explanation is very difficult to interpret. It begins with, "For unless the apostasy comes first, and the rebel (lit. 'the lawless one') is revealed," but then the sentence becomes simply an extended description of "the rebel" and remains unfinished. It should probably be understood as meaning, "For *the end is not here,* unless the apostasy . . ." "Apostasy" refers to the defection of believers. Since some inevitably faltered in the face of persecution, it was commonly accepted that the great "temptation" (testing) at the end would produce considerable apostasy (1 Tim 4:1, cf. Mark 13:13, 20); thus the prayer "Lead us not into [the] temptation [of the last days]" (Matt 6:13).

who restrains is to do so only for the present, until he is removed from the scene. ⁸And then the lawless one will be revealed, whom the Lord [Jesus] will kill with the breath of his mouth and render powerless by the manifestation of his coming, ⁹the one whose coming springs from the power of Satan in

---

The long description of "the rebel, the one doomed to destruction" is reminiscent of various Old Testament texts, most notably Daniel 11:36-37 ("He shall exalt himself, making himself greater than any god"), describing the arrogant King Antiochus, who in 167 B.C. had desecrated the temple sanctuary and viciously persecuted the Jewish people (1 Macc 1:41-63). The whole passage (2 Thess 2:3-9) is full of elements commonly found in apocalyptic texts about the signs of the end of the world: the rebel "seat[ing] himself in the sanctuary" is reminiscent of "the abominating desolation" in Daniel 9:27 (a further reference to King Antiochus) and Mark 13:14, and the theme of deception and apostasy recalls Mark 13:22 (see 1 Tim 4:1 and 2 Tim 4:4). In other words, the writer knows the apocalyptic traditions well and employs them here in full measure to demonstrate, by expert knowledge, that the readers have been deceived. This is not the end of the world! Not yet!

The most difficult problem in this very complex passage is "the restrainer." In verse 6 "what is restraining" (to katechon) is an impersonal (neuter) power, but in verse 7 "it" becomes "he" (ho katechon) who is active "until he *passes from* the scene" (not "is removed"). The New American Bible, along with the majority of scholars, ancient and modern, takes "the restrainer" to be a benevolent power that holds back "the rebel" until the latter is finally "revealed." What or who "the restrainer" is supposed to be is impossible to know; suggestions include the Roman Empire, angelic powers, or the gospel that must be preached to all nations before the end (Matt 24:14). Until that time "the mystery of rebellion is already at work, but only until the restrainer passes away," and then, simultaneously it would seem, "the rebel will [both] be revealed" and will be killed by "the Lord Jesus, with the breath (or Spirit) of his mouth." This "coming" (parousia) of the Lord is the true end for which the readers should wait. This interpretation may be correct, but its major weakness is that "restrainer" may not be the best translation of the Greek term.

An alternative interpretation, found in the notes of the New American Bible, is very different. The Greek word for "the restrainer" (katechon) is ambiguous; elsewhere it usually means "possess" or "seize." If that is the meaning here, then "the possessing power" (katechon) is probably not

every mighty deed and in signs and wonders that lie, [10]and in every wicked deceit for those who are perishing because they have not accepted the love of truth so that they may be saved. [11]Therefore, God is sending them a deceiving power so that they may believe the lie, [12]that all who have not believed the truth but have approved wrongdoing may be condemned.

---

benevolent but is some evil force (person) that anticipates the coming of the final, more terrible evil one. In this case verses 5-7 read:

> Do you not recall that while I was still with you, I told you these things; and now you know the "possessing power," so that the rebel might be revealed in his own time, for the mystery of rebellion is already at work, but let the "possessor" be for the moment, until he passes away.

Believers here are told to wait; "the rebel" will soon enough be revealed and destroyed after the "possessing power passes from the scene." Both interpretations agree that believers are told to wait and hold on to the instruction given long ago. Though now is the *beginning* of the end (see 1 Thess 1:10; 4:13-18), the *end* of the end will be the "coming" *(parousia)* of "the Lord Jesus" and not before. It is impossible to know for sure which interpretation is correct, but overall evidence favors the first.

The passage continues, in tones reminiscent of the harsh words of 1:6 and 8-9, to talk not only of "the lawless one," whose "coming" *(parousia)* "springs from the power of Satan," but also of those who "are perishing, because they have not accepted the love of truth." Though they were deceived by Satan's displays of "power and signs and false wonders" (2:9), the writer insists that they themselves bear responsibility for not accepting the truth. In its reasoning the passage is similar to Romans 1:18-32, which condemns human refusal to "glorify or give thanks" to God, even though knowledge of God was easily available, so that God "gave them up to their passions" and permitted their sins to be their punishment. Here God is envisaged as sending "a deceiving power so that unbelievers might believe the falsehood" and be condemned (2:11-12). Such judgmental, apocalyptic language needs careful evaluation and application. Its rather narrow context is not to be forgotten; certainly a fundamentalist interpretation, which would view all "unbelievers" as necessarily "condemned," would be a misuse of this text. "Love of truth" is a universal value, but complete clarity about "the truth" remains beyond our grasp.

¹³But we ought to give thanks to God for you always, brothers loved by the Lord, because God chose you as the firstfruits for salvation through sanctification by the Spirit and belief in truth. ¹⁴To this end he has [also] called you through our gospel to possess the glory of our Lord Jesus Christ. ¹⁵Therefore, brothers, stand firm and hold fast to the traditions that you were taught, either by an oral statement or by a letter of ours.

¹⁶May our Lord Jesus Christ himself and God our Father, who has loved us and given us everlasting encouragement and good hope through his grace, ¹⁷encourage your hearts and strengthen them in every good deed and word.

2:13-17 A second thanksgiving and prayer

In contrast to the harsh condemnation of unbelievers in 2:10-12, the writer turns to a prayer of thanksgiving for salvation and does so with precisely the same phrase as in 1:3 ("We ought to give thanks to God"). The "choosing" of believers here is a near synonym of God's making them "worthy of the kingdom" (1:5) and "calling" them (1:11). Once again, fully consistent with Paul's own theology, there is a strong emphasis on God's initiative in preparing believers for salvation. "First fruits" (1:13), for Paul himself (e.g., Rom 8:23; 11:16; 1 Cor 15:23), usually suggests the early harvest of something that promises more to come; the meaning here is less clear. It is possible, however, that instead of "first fruits" *(aparchen)*, the text should actually read "from the beginning" *(ap'arches)*, which would emphasize the foresight of God's plan.

In any event, God prepared believers "through sanctification by the Spirit" (God's work) and "belief in truth" (human response). One of the things that distinguishes this letter from 1 Thessalonians is a strong concern with the acceptance of "the truth" (2:10, 12, 13) and the danger of "deceit" (2:9, 11). Neither word is found in 1 Thessalonians. This writer sees "the truth" as coming "through the gospel" (preaching) of Paul and his companions. It is belief in this truth that will lead to possessing "the glory of our Lord Jesus Christ," and therefore believers must "stand firm and hold fast to the [apostolic] traditions" they have received "whether through oral statement or letter" (2:15; cf. 2:2).

The further prayer in 2:16-17 is curiously similar, in a couple of phrases, to that in 1 Thessalonians 3:11-13. The content, however, is different, with this prayer once again emphasizing God's initiative in "loving us [in Christ] and giving eternal consolation and good hope through grace" (2:16). Paul's idea that God enables "every good deed" in believers (2 Cor 8:9) is one that later writers especially liked to repeat (2:17; cf. Eph 2:10; Col 1:10; 2 Tim 3:17).

III. Concluding Exhortations

3 **Request for Prayers.** ¹Finally, brothers, pray for us, so that the word of the Lord may speed forward and be glorified, as it did among you, ²and that we may be delivered from perverse and wicked people, for not all have faith. ³But the Lord is faithful; he will strengthen you and guard you from the evil one. ⁴We are confident of you in the Lord

3:1-16 Final instructions and prayers

In a letter filled with prayers, the writer now asks believers to "pray for us, that the word of the Lord might speed forward (literally 'run') and be glorified" (3:1). There is no way of knowing who "the perverse and wicked persons" (3:2) might be who are envisioned as harassing Paul and his companions. Paul suffered a great deal in his ministry (2 Cor 11:23-33), including in Thessalonica (1 Thess 1:6; Acts 17:5-10), and this writer effectively reminds readers of that fact. That "not all have faith" helps explain this suffering, but "the Lord is faithful who will strengthen you and guard you from the evil one" (3:3). Similarly the writer expresses confidence that the believers are, and will remain, true to the instructions Paul provided, and once again breaks into prayer that "the Lord may direct their hearts" to the greatness of God's love and Christ's endurance in his suffering (3:5).

There follows a lengthy paragraph of instructions that appear to respond to a real situation of Paul's ministry, and some see this as evidence that Paul did indeed write this letter. However, the writer knew 1 Thessalonians and easily reproduces the situation of Paul's letter in order to invoke Paul's authority for the sake of his troubled readers at the end of the first century. Furthermore, though the letter is only fictively addressed to Thessalonica, it is by no means impossible that the very real situation addressed included the kinds of problems identified here. Expectation of the world's imminent end must indeed be a very disruptive experience.

The writer warns the community to avoid any persons who are disruptive and not obedient to "the tradition they received from us" (3:6), once again a focus on apostolic tradition! Believers are to recall Paul's own behavior; he and his companions were models to be imitated. In pursuit of this portrayal, 3:8 borrows both verbally and conceptually from 1 Thessalonians 2:9, that Paul and his co-workers "labored night and day so as to be a burden to no one," in spite of their considerable "authority" (3:9, cf. 1 Thess 2:7). Paul lived out the servant-leadership of Jesus (Mark 10:42-45; John 13:12-14) and is thus a model to be imitated (3:9).

that what we instruct you, you [both] are doing and will continue to do. [5]May the Lord direct your hearts to the love of God and to the endurance of Christ.

Neglect of Work. [6]We instruct you, brothers, in the name of [our] Lord Jesus Christ, to shun any brother who conducts himself in a disorderly way and not according to the tradition they received from us. [7]For you know how one must imitate us. For we did not act in a disorderly way among you, [8]nor did we eat food received free from anyone. On the contrary, in toil and drudgery, night and day we worked, so as not to burden any of you. [9]Not that we do not have the right. Rather, we

wanted to present ourselves as a model for you, so that you might imitate us. [10]In fact, when we were with you, we instructed you that if anyone was unwilling to work, neither should that one eat. [11]We hear that some are conducting themselves among you in a disorderly way, by not keeping busy but minding the business of others. [12]Such people we instruct and urge in the Lord Jesus Christ to work quietly and to eat their own food. [13]But you, brothers, do not be remiss in doing good. [14]If anyone does not obey our word as expressed in this letter, take note of this person not to associate with him, that he may be put to shame. [15]Do

The injunction that "if anyone is unwilling to work, neither should that one eat," (3:10) is quite believable as a tradition that might have come from Paul, given his own self-reliance. It is probably also an allusion to sharing all things in common (Acts 2:44). What the writer is primarily concerned about is the "disorderly" conduct of those who are not doing productive work (3:11) but are being busybodies, perhaps fomenting speculation about the end of the world. Such people are solemnly warned that they are to "work quietly and eat their own food" (3:12). The community as a whole is to persevere in doing good (3:13).

There follows a solemn instruction to the community that "if anyone does not obey our word through this letter, [they are to] take note of, and not associate with, such a person" (3:14). This harsh treatment, however, does not mean they are to excommunicate the person permanently. The language here recalls Paul's instruction in 1 Corinthians 5:9 regarding believers who were guilty of serious immorality. The instruction "Do not regard the offender as an enemy, but warn as speaking to a brother or sister" (3:15) also recalls Matthew 18:15-18, where a process is established for dealing with offenses and reconciliation within church communities. It is instructive to recall that these are the origins of the sacrament of reconciliation, with private confessionals not originating until many centuries later. The paragraph closes with yet another prayer that "the Lord of peace give you peace always and in every way."

not regard him as an enemy but admonish him as a brother. [16]May the Lord of peace himself give you peace at all times and in every way. The Lord be with all of you.

IV. Final Greetings

[17]This greeting is in my own hand, Paul's. This is the sign in every letter; this is how I write. [18]The grace of our Lord Jesus Christ be with all of you.

3:17-18 Further "proof" of Paul's authority and final blessing

In conclusion the writer tries very hard—one might say, too hard—to convince the readers that this letter indeed derives from Paul himself (3:17). His purpose, of course, is to appeal to Paul's authority in order to reassure churches that are suffering in very difficult persecutions and need encouragement and instruction. Paul himself did authenticate his letters with his own handwriting (2 Cor 16:21; Gal 6:11; Phlm 19), but never three times over! The text, however, is Sacred Scripture, regardless of its author, as is also true of other biblical texts. The Scriptures arise from the church and from the faith of believers, and the church did not disappear with the deaths of the apostles. This letter arises from a church that is suffering and witnesses that, even in the absence of Paul, believers held onto faith and enabled the church to grow.

The final blessing (3:18, "The grace of our Lord Jesus Christ be with you all") corresponds with Paul's standard final words in his letters (e.g., 1 Thess 5:28; 1 Cor 16:23; Gal 6:18) and is now used in the liturgy.

The Letter to the Colossians

Colossians among Paul's letters

Among the thirteen letters that bear Paul's name, Colossians has a unique place. Seven letters are universally accepted as written by Paul (Romans, 1 and 2 Corinthians, Galatians, Philippians, 1 Thessalonians, Philemon). A large majority think that Paul did not write the Pastoral Letters (1 and 2 Timothy, Titus) or Ephesians, and a growing majority think the same regarding 2 Thessalonians. That leaves Colossians. A small majority favor the conclusion that Paul himself is not the author, but a number of them think that Paul was still alive and may have had some say in the letter's composition. In this case, someone like Timothy was the main author, with Paul providing input. Just about all would agree with one author's description of Colossians as a "bridge" between Paul himself and those who continued his ministry and wrote further letters in his name.

Colossians certainly bears many striking similarities to Paul's letters, but with regard to style and theology and the absence of some key Pauline terms (e.g., "righteousness," "law," addressing the readers as "brothers"), its distinctiveness is very apparent. The image of Christ and the church as cosmic entities is particularly distinctive, as also is the style of lengthy sentences overflowing with synonymous expressions. Whoever wrote Colossians knew Paul's letters, and perhaps Paul himself, quite well but also had developed a unique style and theological view. Paul sometimes wrote in the name of his co-workers; here one of them or someone associated with them has written in Paul's name.

The close connections between Colossians and Ephesians will be discussed in the commentary on Ephesians (see pp. 92 and 108).

When and why was Colossians written?

A reasonable hypothesis is that the letter was written from Ephesus, perhaps while Paul was in prison in Rome or shortly after his death (i.e., early to late sixties A.D.). It has two main purposes: first, to respond to the challenge presented by "the philosophy" (2:8), and second, to provide some support for Epaphras (1:7; 4:12-13) and others in their furthering of Paul's ministry. "The philosophy" probably had its home in Judaism (note 2:11, 16, 21) and invoked ideas from popular philosophy, such as "the elements of the world" (2:8), which were identified with spiritual "powers" (2:10, 15, 18). Colossians has none of the polemic of Galatians, but as in that case, the law was being introduced as a necessary factor between believers and God, as though the divine-human relationship required a legal code (see 2:13-15). Like Paul in Galatians, this writer insists that believers live "in Christ" (2:7) and indeed "in God" (3:3) and have no need of any such intervening power (cf. Gal 2:19-21).

The value of Colossians for today is in that teaching. Believers in every generation need to remember that nothing is to displace the primacy of a direct relationship with God "in Christ."

The Letter to the Colossians

I. Address

Greeting. ¹Paul, an apostle of Christ Jesus by the will of God, and Timothy our brother, ²to the holy ones and faithful brothers in Christ in Colossae: grace to you and peace from God our Father.

◄ **Thanksgiving.** ³We always give thanks to God, the Father of our Lord Jesus Christ, when we pray for you,

⁴for we have heard of your faith in Christ Jesus and the love that you have for all the holy ones ⁵because of the hope reserved for you in heaven. Of this you have already heard through the word of truth, the gospel, ⁶that has come to you. Just as in the whole world it is bearing fruit and growing, so also among you, from the day you heard it and came to know the grace of God in

1:1-2 Opening greeting

The opening verse is identical to the opening words of 2 Corinthians 1:1. In Corinth (1 Cor 9:1-5; 2 Cor 11:5-33) and in Galatia (Gal 1:1–2:14), Paul had to defend his apostolate. In Colossae his apostolate seems to have been unchallenged, but the words "apostle of Christ Jesus by the will of God" might have been necessary because the Colossian churches did not know him by sight (2:1) and also he wanted to make more effective the commendation of those who would continue his ministry (1:7; 4:7-14). Timothy had long been a major partner in Paul's mission (1 Thess 1:1; 3:2; Acts 16:1-3). Although the addressees are "the believers in Colossae" (1:2), the letter is intended also for other churches (4:13-15). The greeting here is shorter than usual (cf. Rom 1:7; 1 Cor 1:3).

1:3-8 Thanksgiving

In Greek this thanksgiving comprises just one sentence. Generally, it echoes Paul's thought and language well; "giving thanks," "praying," and recalling of the recipients' coming to faith are all characteristic of Paul's thanksgivings (e.g., Phil 1:3-5; 1 Thess 1:2-5). Further, faith, love, and hope are featured here, as in 1 Thessalonians, but whereas, for Paul, hope is a quality that enables "eager expectation" for the coming reward

► This symbol indicates a cross reference number in the *Catechism of the Catholic Church*. See page 123 for number citations.

truth, [7]as you learned it from Epaphras our beloved fellow slave, who is a trustworthy minister of Christ on your behalf [8]and who also told us of your love in the Spirit.

Prayer for Continued Progress. [9]Therefore, from the day we heard this, we do not cease praying for you and asking that you may be filled with the knowledge of his will through all spiritual wisdom and understanding [10]to live in a manner worthy of the Lord, so as to be fully pleasing, in every good work bearing fruit and growing in the

(Rom 8:18-25; Phil 1:20), here it suggests not expectation but the reward itself "reserved for you in heaven" (1:5).

The Colossians "heard" the gospel from Epaphras and recognized in it "the grace of God." Epaphras had established the church in Colossae (1:7-8; 4:12-13) and had been imprisoned with Paul (Phlm 23); he also provided the news of the Colossians' faith (their "love in the Spirit") and (probably) of the competing "philosophy" (2:8). The strong commendation ("our beloved fellow slave . . .") unites Epaphras closely with Paul, confirming his fidelity to Christ *"on your behalf"* (cf. 1:24; 2:1); the latter phrase is otherwise used most often of *Christ's* sacrifice (e.g., Rom 5:8; 8:32; 1 Cor 11:24). The gospel, says the writer, "has come to you" and indeed to "the whole world," something of an exaggeration in the first century (1:23)! In any event, the gospel is "bearing fruit" among the Colossians (1:6); the writer is not fearful for them (2:5), as Paul was for the Galatians (Gal 4:11).

1:9-14 Prayer for the Colossians

This section also comprises one long sentence. It describes an enthusiastic prayer for the Colossians' growth in faith. "From the day" Paul and his companions "heard" about it, they have been praying (the verbs express continuous action) that the Colossians "might be filled" with all necessary spiritual gifts (1:9-11). There is a strong emphasis on gifts of "knowledge" and "wisdom" (1:9-10), which goes along with this letter's contesting of "a philosophy" (2:8) and with the description of Paul and his companions as those who "teach with all wisdom" (1:28). Faith has everything to do with commitment and right action, another strong emphasis of this letter (1:10, 21-22; 3:1–4:6), but faith must also be intelligent both to direct behavior (2:16-23) and for the sake of witness to outsiders (4:5-6). Behavior and knowledge are virtually inseparable (1:10).

The second half of the prayer shows that *what* believers "know" goes far beyond mere intellectual knowledge; it has to do with knowing the dignity that God bestows on believers, already granting them "a share with the saints in light" and transferring them "to the kingdom of his

knowledge of God, [11]strengthened with every power, in accord with his glorious might, for all endurance and patience, with joy [12]giving thanks to the Father, who has made you fit to share in the inheritance of the holy ones in light. [13]He delivered us from the power of darkness and transferred us to the kingdom of his beloved Son, [14]in whom we have redemption, the forgiveness of sins.

II. The Preeminence of Christ

His Person and Work

[15]He is the image of the invisible God, the firstborn of all creation.
[16]For in him were created all things in heaven and on earth, the visible and the invisible, whether thrones or dominions or principalities or powers; all things were created through him and for him.

---

beloved Son" (1:12-13). Such language of future blessings realized *now* contrasts with Paul's own theology (2:12; 3:1, cf. Rom 6:5), but it reminds the Colossians that "the reality" is already theirs (2:17).

The prayer witnesses to the charismatic enthusiasm that also characterized Paul's experience of church prayer (e.g., 1 Cor 14:1-19). It conveys the thankful "joy" (1:11-12) of being in Christ; "in him" they "have redemption, the forgiveness of sins" (1:14). "Forgiveness" is virtually unmentioned in Paul's own letters (only Rom 4:7). Paul's theology deals more with God's *gifts* in Christ (Spirit, freedom, adoption) than with sins removed. Here the prayer, which has become a celebratory recounting of God's action (1:12-14), prepares for a glorious hymn in praise of the cosmic Christ.

1:15-20 The cosmic Christ

These verses encapsulate a hymn or spiritual song (3:16, cf. John 1:1-18; Phil 2:6-11), older than the letter itself, that was incorporated here, with a few editorial touches, by the letter's author. As it stands, it has two main parts: describing Christ's role in creation (1:15-17) and in reconciliation (1:18-20). Its editing is not easily distinguished from the original. Still, scholars have ventured some educated guesses, which can illustrate the kind of development that may account for this difficult but profound text.

1. "Of the church" (1:18a) breaks the established rhythm and restricts "all things" to "the church." Probably "the head of the body" originally envisaged "the body" of *creation*, applying to Christ language that, in the wider Greco-Roman culture, was sometimes used of Zeus. "Of the church" was added to prepare for subsequent teaching (2:19).

2. In 1:16b the "powers" listed correspond precisely to the "powers" which are a part of the competing teaching and which God "stripped

[17]He is before all things,
    and in him all things hold
        together.
[18]He is the head of the body, the
        church.
He is the beginning, the firstborn
        from the dead,
    that in all things he himself might
        be preeminent.
	[19]For in him all the fullness was
	        pleased to dwell,
	[20]and through him to reconcile
	        all things for him,
	making peace by the blood of his
	        cross
	[through him], whether those
	        on earth or those in
	        heaven.

away" and defeated (2:8-10, 15). They may have been added to 1:16 to emphasize their subordination to Christ.

3. Probably the hymn originally spoke of God ("the fullness," cf. 2:9), by means of Christ's *resurrection* ("the firstborn from the dead," 1:18), "reconciling all things through him" (1:20; cf. 2 Cor 5:18-19). The reference to Christ's death ("the blood of his cross") *after* the resurrection is awkward and looks like an editorial addition.

It is reasonable to think that the original hymn might have looked something like the following. If the bracketed lines are omitted, we end up with two stanzas of four lines each (italicized text); one theory does just that and *could* be correct.

> 1:15 *He is the image of the invisible God* (2 Cor 4:4),
> *firstborn of all creation* (Prov 8:22-31; Rev 3:14),
> [16] *for in him all things were created* (1 Cor 8:6; John 1:3)
> (in the heavens and upon the earth) (Phil 2:10)
> *all things were created through him and for him* (cf. Rom 11:36)
> [17] (and he is before all things
> and all things hold together in him
> [18a] and he is the head of the body). (Eph 4:15)
> [18b] *He is the beginning,*
> *firstborn from the dead* (1 Cor 15:20),
> (that he might be the first among all)
> [19] *for in him all the fullness was pleased to dwell* (2:9-10)
> [20] *and through him to reconcile all things* (2 Cor 5:18-19),
> (whether things on earth or things in heaven).

As edited by the letter writer, this was a Christian hymn, but several scholars maintain, with good reason, that it was either modeled on an earlier Jewish hymn in praise of Wisdom (cf. Prov 8:22-31) or was inspired by applying Wisdom traditions to Christ (e.g., Wis 7:22-30), as in John 1:1-18.

Seniors in Turkey passing the time of day

²¹And you who once were alienated and hostile in mind because of evil deeds ²²he has now reconciled in his fleshly body through his death, to present you holy, without blemish, and irreproachable before him, ²³provided

---

The hymn was adapted to provide a theological base from which to fight "the philosophy" (2:8). If we could know this (probably Jewish) "philosophy" as the Colossians did, we would, undoubtedly, recognize some measure of sincerity and goodness in its teachers. Paul had described even Peter as "clearly wrong" and a "hypocrite" (Gal 2:12-14); so here, these teachers are described in negative terms (2:8, 18) but were not necessarily evil. Nevertheless, their teaching compromises the gospel. It seems to have involved "the elements of the world" (2:8, 20), "the principalities and powers" (2:10, 15), which humans were to obey by certain ascetic practices (2:21-23). However, the fault was not asceticism (note Matt 6:16-18; 1 Cor 7:29-35), but requiring trust to be placed in "principalities," as though they could produce what Christ had *already* accomplished. The "powers" were, in effect, becoming rivals of Christ.

The hymn, therefore, makes clear that Christ is the ruler of the *cosmos*; all powers, including angels (2:18), are subject to him. He is "the image of the invisible God, the firstborn of all creation" (1:15). The hymn has a very high view of the divinity of Christ, but it is a step in the development of doctrine, not its completion; it has not reached the level of the Nicene Creed. And yet, in both parts of the hymn (1:15, 18), Christ is supreme over creation, both its agent and its goal (1:16), the one in whom "all things hold together" (1:17). What elsewhere is said of God (Rom 11:36) is ascribed here to Christ (1:16d), who is clearly understood as preexistent before the rest of creation (1:17-18).

It is very important in this letter that Christ is "the head" not only of creation but also "of the church" (1:18). "The church" here, like Christ, is a cosmic entity, since it is "his body" (1:24). The major focus, however, remains on Christ; "in him all the fullness was pleased to dwell and, through him [Christ] to reconcile all things to him" (i.e., "to God," 2 Cor 5:19, but see 1:22). "The fullness" evidently refers to God (cf. 2:9), or at least that's the way the writer of the letter sees it. In the original it might simply have referred to "the fullness" of spiritual reality (cf. John 1:14, 16). "Fullness" is an important concept in both Colossians and Ephesians (Eph 1:23). As Christ bears "the fullness" of God, so believers are to "be filled with all the fullness of God" and "of Christ" (Col 2:9; Eph 3:19; 4:13).

that you persevere in the faith, firmly grounded, stable, and not shifting from the hope of the gospel that you heard,	which has been preached to every creature under heaven, of which I, Paul, am a minister.

"Reconciliation," though using a slightly different Greek word, was also important in Paul's own letters (Rom 5:10-11; 2 Cor 5:18-20). There, as here, it denotes God's action in and through Christ, but whereas "the world," for Paul (2 Cor 5:19), meant simply human beings, estranged by sin from God (e.g., Rom 5:12; cf. Col 1:22), here "all things" includes the universe itself, which the ancient world sometimes saw as out of balance. They admired its beauty and order, but natural and moral evils suggested that the "body" of the *cosmos* needed the *logos* of God—reconciliation. Once again, this answers "the philosophy"; believers do not need lesser authorities ("the principalities and powers"). In Christ "the head," God has "reconciled all things" (1:20), including by "the blood of his cross" (cf. 2:14-15!).

1:21-23 The meaning of the hymn for Colossae

The amended hymn is immediately applied to the Colossians; they once were "alienated" (from God) and "hostile in mind." "Mind" has more to do with attitude than with intellect; proper "understanding" in that broader and deeper sense is crucial (e.g. 1:9-10). "Evil deeds" (1:21) are both the cause and the demonstration of minds out of tune with God (cf. Rom 1:18-32). "But now" (cf. Rom 3:21; 6:22) Christ has "reconciled" them "in his fleshly body through death" (1:22). "Fleshly body" (cf. 2:11) is a strange phrase; both terms were important for Paul (e.g., Rom 6:6, 12; 7:4; 1 Cor 12:13, 27; Rom 7:5; 8:3), but he never combined them as here. In the present context "body" recalls, and contrasts with, 1:18. The cosmic Christ is "head" of both the universe and the church, but Jesus, in his own *"fleshly* body through death," achieved reconciliation. In baptism believers "strip off" the "fleshly body" (2:11).

Christ's purpose is to "present" the reconciled before God (cf. 1:28) like a "holy, unblemished" sacrifice (cf. Rom 12:1), "irreproachable" at the judgment (1:22) in spite of their sinful past. They, of course, must "persevere in the faith"; all is not yet complete. They must remain "firmly grounded, not shifting from the hope" that the gospel produced. The gospel of the cosmic Christ has been "proclaimed in all creation under heaven," a considerable exaggeration (as in 1:6), but aiming to demonstrate that the gospel, contrary to "the philosophy," is in accordance with God's plan for

Christ in Us. [24]Now I rejoice in my sufferings for your sake, and in my flesh I am filling up what is lacking in the afflictions of Christ on behalf of his body, which is the church, [25]of which I am a minister in accordance with God's stewardship given to me to bring to completion for you the word of God, [26]the mystery hidden from ages and from generations past. But now it has been manifested to his holy ones, [27]to whom God chose to make known the riches of the glory of this mystery among the Gentiles; it is Christ in you, the hope for glory. [28]It is he whom we proclaim, admonishing everyone and teaching everyone with all wisdom, that we may present everyone perfect in Christ. [29]For this I labor and struggle, in accord with the exercise of his power working within me.

2 [1]For I want you to know how great a struggle I am having for you and for those in Laodicea and all who have

---

the universe "from all eternity" (1:25-26). This exaltation of the gospel, and of Paul as its "minister" (*diakonos*—cf. 1:25), goes beyond anything that Paul himself said (cf. Rom 1:16-17; 15:19), but it furthers the Colossians' idea of Christ and the church as cosmic entities. It also prepares for the next section.

1:24–2:5 Paul, his co-workers, and God's eternal plan

If Colossians was written, in part, to establish the authority of those who continued Paul's ministry, this purpose is largely accomplished here. To "rejoice in sufferings" echoes Paul's tendency to see suffering, and even death, as nothing in comparison with the joy of being in Christ (e.g., Rom 8:18; Phil 1:19-23). The following claim for Paul's sufferings, as "completing what is lacking [!] in the afflictions of Christ" (1:24), is surprising and, on the face of it, shocking. The notion that somehow Christ's death might be inadequate was anathema to Paul (Gal 2:21); it is inconceivable that such a claim is intended here. Rather, dwelling on Paul's thoughts about his sufferings as an apostle (especially 2 Cor 4:7-10), the writer sees them as having a role "for your sake . . . on behalf of [Christ's] body, the church," which, like all creation, continues to "groan" as it awaits "the redemption of our bodies" (Rom 8:18-25). It might be, as one author has suggested, that the crucial phrase should be hyphenated: "I am completing what is lacking in *Christ's-afflictions-in-my-flesh* for the sake of his body." In this case, it is not Christ's own sufferings that might be lacking, but rather the sufferings of Paul for the sake of Christ and the church.

This emotional recalling of Paul's sufferings "for your sake" and the reminder that he was the church's "minister according to God's steward-

not seen me face to face, [2]that their hearts may be encouraged as they are brought together in love, to have all the richness of fully assured understanding, for the knowledge of the mystery of God, Christ, [3]in whom are hidden all the treasures of wisdom and knowledge.

III. Warnings Against False Teachers

A General Admonition. [4]I say this so that no one may deceive you by specious arguments. [5]For even if I am absent in the flesh, yet I am with you in spirit, rejoicing as I observe your good order and the firmness of your faith in

---

ship" (1:25) shed a favorable light also on Paul's co-workers, "we" who aid him in "proclaiming" and "instructing" (1:28). "We," strongly emphasized in the Greek, includes Timothy, Epaphras, and Tychicus (1:1, 7-8; 4:7-14). Paul had "fulfilled for you the word of God," the word that was an ancient and "hidden mystery, but now is manifested to God's holy ones" (1:26). "Holy ones" (cf. 1:2) denotes *all* the baptized, but here there is some emphasis on the preachers.

"Hidden mystery" is apocalyptic language. "Apocalypse" is the Greek word for "revelation," and in apocalyptic literature (especially Daniel and Revelation; cf. Mark 13; Matt 24), God's ancient plan for the world is "revealed" to a seer (Daniel, Enoch, John, the apostles), who then imparts it to others through speech or writing (e.g., Dan 2:19-28; cf. 7:1-28; Rev 1:1, 9-11). The plan ultimately always has to do with the *eschaton*, the end of the world ("the hope of glory," 1:27). However, here the expectation of the end is not as imminent as for Paul himself (e.g., 1 Cor 7:29-31; 1 Thess 4:13-17), though it has not disappeared, as it mostly has today.

Colossians strikes a wonderful balance: the "mystery" is "Christ in you," an experience here and now that anticipates "the glory" hoped for. The apostles proclaim the gospel "so that," at the judgment, they will be able to "present everyone perfect in Christ" (cf. 1:22; Phil 2:16). That was the reason for Paul's "labor and struggle," and that, indeed, was the purpose of Christ's "power working within me" (1:29).

As there is a strong emphasis on the "power" of Christ at work within Paul (1:29), so there is also emphasis on his "struggle for your sake (cf. 1:24) and for those in Laodicea" (2:1). Epaphras (1:7-8) had acted as Paul's emissary, but Paul remained the key authority. Paul's concern for his churches (see 2 Cor 11:28) was important to emphasize, especially for those who had never known him personally (2:1). His struggle had been for their encouragement, their "unity in love," and, returning to a prominent theme, their "understanding" (cf. 1:9-10). Neither Paul nor his co-workers own and control the gospel; their purpose is that believers attain

Christ. ⁶So, as you received Christ Jesus the Lord, walk in him, ⁷rooted in him and built upon him and established in the faith as you were taught, abounding in thanksgiving. ⁸See to it that no one captivate you with an empty, seductive philosophy according to human tradition, according to the elemental powers of the world and not according to Christ.

"all the richness of fully assured understanding and knowledge" (2:2). It is the entire community that is to understand "the mystery of God, Christ."

"Mystery" recalls 1:27 (above). The phrase "God, Christ" is confusing; the ancient manuscript copiers produced fifteen variations on this phrase in their attempts to explain it (e.g., "God the Father," "God, the Father of Christ")! It is not impossible that Christ is called "God" here, but "the God of Christ" (cf. 1:3; 2 Cor 1:3) is also possible, or perhaps the thought is that "Christ" is the content of "God's mystery." This goes along well with "the mystery, which is Christ in you" (1:27) and is perhaps the best we can do. In any event, it is "in him" that "all the treasures of wisdom and knowledge are hidden" (2:3), and therefore for believers they are not hidden at all (cf. 2 Cor 4:1-6).

The writer hints for the first time at the presence of some threatening ideas. Their "knowledge" of Christ should keep them safe from seemingly persuasive but actually "specious arguments" (2:4). Though Paul cannot be with them "in the flesh," he is with them "in the spirit" (cf. 1 Cor 5:3). If he were with them, he would rejoice at "the strength" of their "faith in Christ" (2:5). The writer's confidence, in spite of the threat, is notable.

2:6–3:4 Hold to "the faith"; no further "philosophy" is needed

The writer now turns to countering the threat of alternative ideas, doing so first by general encouragement that sets the theme for the major sections to come. Just as they "received Christ" and were "rooted and established in him," so they must "walk" (2:6-7). There is first a constant reminder of what believers *already have* in Christ and why no further teachings or dictates (2:14, 20) are required. "The faith" here denotes *what* "you were taught," the message as preached by Epaphras (1:7), but faith as *trust* and *relationship* (2:5) is by no means separate from the message (cf. Rom 10:9), an important point for the church today. Faith in its fullness leads naturally to fullness of "thanksgiving" (*eucharistia*, 2:7).

Whether the writer has a specific "someone" in mind is difficult to say (see 2:16-18). Certainly there is no one in Colossae comparable to the

◄ **Sovereign Role of Christ.** ⁹For in
him dwells the whole fullness of the
deity bodily, ¹⁰and you share in this
fullness in him, who is the head of
every principality and power. ¹¹In him ►
you were also circumcised with a circumcision not administered by hand,
by stripping off the carnal body, with

---

opponents in Galatia (Gal 1:7). Nevertheless, there is the seductive power
of some "philosophy," which the writer regards as based in "human tradition," having to do with "the elementary powers of the world" (2:8, 10, 15;
cf. 1:21). The "elements" (earth, air, fire, water) were widely thought to be
the foundational components of the universe and were sometimes regarded as personal forces (e.g., Wis 13:2; Gal 4:3; 2 Pet 3:10-12); in Judaism
they could be associated with angels and the giving of the law (Acts 7:53;
Gal 3:19; 4:9-10).

The attraction of such teaching is that it takes seriously the invisible
and unpredictable "powers" that affect human existence. Further, it pre-
scribes practices (2:21), in the manner of the sacred laws of Judaism, for
dealing with those forces. In this regard there is a link between the problem envisioned here and that in Galatia. And, as in Galatia, the solution is
to recall the status already attained in Christ (e.g., Gal 4:1-7). Thus whatever is "not according to Christ" is to be rejected (2:8; cf. Gal 5:2-4).

"In him"—the tenth occurrence of this idea so far—"dwells the whole
fullness of the deity bodily" (2:9), a very strong statement of Christ's identity with God (cf. 1:19; John 1:1, 14). The present tense is important; this
was not merely something that happened in the past, when Christ was on
earth. It is true now, and believers, who are "in Christ," already "share in
this fullness" of divinity (2:10; cf. John 17:20-23). There can be no improve-
ment, says Colossians, on Christ as the means of access to God. Christ is
"the head of every principality"; the "elements" have nothing to add.

The next paragraph employs a series of metaphors, focused largely
around baptism, to bring out the meaning of being "in him." Jewish writers sometimes spoke of "circumcision" as the "stripping away" of vice;
circumcision ultimately had to involve the "circumcision of the heart"
(Deut 30:6, cf. Rom 2:29). Such circumcision "was not administered by
hand." The "stripping off of the fleshly body" (cf. 1:22) could be achieved
only "by the circumcision of Christ," that is "by baptism." In baptism believers were "buried with" Christ and even "raised with" him "by faith in
the power of God." (2:12). That believers are *already* "raised" goes notably
beyond what Paul himself said (cf. Rom 6:5; 8:11; 2 Cor 4:14), but it makes
the point about what believers have in Christ.

the circumcision of Christ. [12]You were buried with him in baptism, in which you were also raised with him through faith in the power of God, who raised him from the dead. [13]And even when you were dead [in] transgressions and the uncircumcision of your flesh, he brought you to life along with him, having forgiven us all our transgressions; [14]obliterating the bond against us, with its legal claims, which was opposed to us, he also removed it from our midst, nailing it to the cross; [15]despoiling the principalities and the powers, he made a public spectacle of them, leading them away in triumph by it.

Practices Contrary to Faith. [16]Let no one, then, pass judgment on you in matters of food and drink or with re-

The baptismal imagery continues, employing perhaps language of the liturgy and highlighting the transformation from a life "dead in transgressions" (Eph 2:1) to one in which God "brought you to life with him" (cf. Rom 6:4), "forgiving us all our transgressions" (2:13; cf. 1:14). These are already vivid metaphors, but now they pile up even further, going beyond the language of baptism. Verses 14-15 contain six verbs ("obliterating," "removed," "nailing," "despoiling," "made a spectacle" and "leading in triumph"). Presumably their subject, following the sequence from 1:13, is God rather than Christ. It is also possible that the writer is content to be ambiguous, permitting the imagery to have its effect regardless. Probably at least 1:14 describes God's action.

God "obliterated the bond" that, with its "legal claims," held sinful humans in debt. "The bond" is the legal document listing human failures. The image is like the slave with the impossible debt in Jesus' parable (Matt 18:21-35). When human behavior is stacked beside the demands of the law, then humans deserve condemnation. In freeing humans, God did not obliterate the law—the law is "holy" (Rom 7:12)—but rather the condemnation that it produces (cf. Rom 8:1-4). God "removed [the bond] from our midst, nailing it to the cross" (2:14), a powerful way to speak of God in Christ making peace with the world (1:20, 22; 2 Cor 5:18). If God is the subject, then "in him" (not "by it") God "despoiled," more literally *"stripped away*, the principalities and powers, made a public spectacle of them, and paraded them" in a victorious procession, like a general with prisoners of war (2:15).

It would, therefore, be nonsense for believers to revert to a position from which God has set them free (cf. Gal 4:8-10) and permit anyone to "pass judgment" on them with regard to religious rules and regulations (2:16). Such things are "a shadow" in comparison with "the substance," literally "the *body* of Christ" (2:17; cf. 1:24). The word "disqualify" is re-

is this stating a new comment re.sabbath.

gard to a festival or new moon or sabbath. ¹⁷These are shadows of things to come; the reality belongs to Christ. ¹⁸Let no one disqualify you, delighting in self-abasement and worship of angels, taking his stand on visions, inflated without reason by his fleshly mind, ¹⁹and not holding closely to the head, from whom the whole body, supported and held together by its liga-

ments and bonds, achieves the growth that comes from God.

²⁰If you died with Christ to the elemental powers of the world, why do you submit to regulations as if you were still living in the world? ²¹"Do not handle! Do not taste! Do not touch!" ²²These are all things destined to perish with use; they accord with human precepts and teachings. ²³While they have

lated to the word for "prize" in Philippians 3:14, but here the thought is that someone might "deny [believers] the prize" of being "in God" (3:3).

There is further difficult use of multiple images with no agreement on precisely what the writer means. In discussion with the competing philosophy, some advantage seems to have been claimed for ascetic practices (cf. 1:23) that enable "self-abasement" ("humility," cf. 3:12) not only by obeying regulations but also by "the worship of angels," meaning probably by being able to *join in with* "the worship of angels" (cf. Isa 6:2-3; Dan 7:10; Rev 4:9-10; 7:11-12). This is what the "visions" were probably about as the person was "entering into" worship (not "taking his stand"). The claims made were probably impressive and attractive.

The writer, however, is quite scathing in evaluating these claims, whatever they are. Such a person is "inflated [conceited] without reason," not genuinely "humble" at all (cf. Phil 2:1-5). This is not true spiritual understanding but suggests only "a fleshly mind" (2:18). Such a person— a believer is envisaged—ought rather to "hold on to the head" (1:18; 2:10), who alone guarantees the proper "support" and "growth" of the body (2:19). The main point is repeated and emphasized: if believers "died with Christ" (cf. 2:11-12; Rom 6:2, 8), being liberated "from the elements," it is nonsense to return to "regulations." Far from taking believers into heavenly worship, that only projects them back into the insecurities of "living in [this] world" (2:20, cf. 3:1); they are back again to being dictated to, and "the glorious freedom of the children of God" (Rom 8:21) is lost!

The divine-human relationship does not rest on law but on God's love and compassion (Rom 5:6-8; 9:16; Gal 2:11-21). Regulations have a place; this writer will soon provide more than enough (3:18–4:1)! But such rules ("Don't touch, don't eat"), like the things they deal with, "are bound for destruction"; ultimately they are only "human precepts" (2:22; cf. Mark 7:7). They have "a semblance of wisdom," a passing usefulness (2:23), but

a semblance of wisdom in rigor of devotion and self-abasement [and] severity to the body, they are of no value against gratification of the flesh.

IV. The Ideal Christian Life in the World

Mystical Death and Resurrection. 3 ¹If then you were raised with Christ, seek what is above, where Christ is seated at the right hand of God. ²Think of what is above, not of what is on earth. ³For you have died, and your life is hidden with Christ in God. ⁴When Christ your life appears, then you too will appear with him in glory.

Renunciation of Vice. ⁵Put to death, then, the parts of you that are earthly: immorality, impurity, passion, evil desire, and the greed that is idolatry.

Jesus did not come with a system of law—"the sabbath is for people, not people for the sabbath" (Mark 2:27). In any context, ancient or modern, this is quite a radical stance and by no means easily maintained. It nevertheless reflects well both Jesus and Paul.

In conclusion, believers "were raised with Christ" (3:1; cf. 2:12), who is "seated at God's right hand" (3:1; cf. Ps 110; Matt 22:44; Acts 2:34; 1 Cor 15:25). Their focus is not to be on "things of earth" (3:2), religion and rules that skew the relationship with God. Having "died" with Christ (cf. Gal 2:19-20), the "life" of the baptized is now "hidden with Christ in God" (3:3). "Hidden" evokes God's ancient "mystery" and "wisdom" (2:3) manifested to believers (1:26-27), but now believers are themselves a *part of the mystery*, so that at the end, "when Christ, your life, appears," they also "will appear with him in glory" (3:4). Why bother with "angels" when you already commune with God?

3:5-17 Reject evil, do good

Having reminded believers that they "died and were raised with Christ" (2:12, 20; 3:1), the author now tells them to "put to death the parts of you that are earthly" (3:5). Now the rubber, so to speak, hits the road: believers do in fact "live in the world" (2:20) and indeed "in the flesh" (cf. 2:23)! Paul himself had faced the same irony (e.g., Gal 5:1, 13-17). Though believers have "stripped off the old self . . . and put on the new" (3:9-10), they remain "in the flesh" (Gal 2:20), and its temptations are always at hand (see Rom 8:3-8). God's reconciling of humans does not eliminate their freedom or their capacity to reject goodness.

The first list of vices (3:5) centers mostly on sexual sins (cf. 1 Thess 4:3-4) but culminates with "greed," which some ancient writers regarded as among the worst evils (cf. Luke 12:15). Here it is equated with "idolatry." Such things earn "the wrath of God" (cf. Rom 1:18). The Colossians are

⁶Because of these the wrath of God is coming [upon the disobedient]. ⁷By these you too once conducted yourselves, when you lived in that way. ⁸But now you must put them all away: anger, fury, malice, slander, and obscene language out of your mouths. ⁹Stop lying to one another, since you have taken off the old self with its practices ¹⁰and have put on the new self, which is being renewed, for knowledge, in the image of its creator. ¹¹Here there is not Greek and Jew, circumcision and uncircumcision, barbarian, Scythian, slave, free; but Christ is all and in all.

¹²Put on then, as God's chosen ones, holy and beloved, heartfelt compassion, kindness, humility, gentleness, and patience, ¹³bearing with one another and forgiving one another, if one

again reminded (cf. 2:13) that their own lives were once characterized by such vices, but now "they must put them all away"; there follows a further list centering on vices that disrupt friendship and community, culminating with the command to "stop lying."

The language next recalls baptism (cf. 2:11-12) and, as earlier, uses the metaphor of "stripping off." Baptism involved disrobing before entering into the baptismal pool and then "putting on" a new garment to symbolize "putting on Christ" (Gal 3:27; Rom 13:14). The "new self," says the writer, "is *being* renewed [an *ongoing* process!] for knowledge (cf. 2:3), according to the image of its creator" (3:10; cf. 1:15; Gen 1:26-27). It is not just a matter of virtues but of an entirely "new self," "new creation" (2 Cor 5:17). As the perversion of "knowledge" had distorted humanity (Rom 1:18-23), so genuine knowledge will characterize the new humanity.

Baptismal language continues. Apparently, in Paul's churches the baptismal formula included something like "In Christ there is no longer Greek and Jew" (3:11; cf. 1 Cor 12:13; Gal 3:28). This expressed succinctly the new reality created in baptism and experienced within the church, where all races, classes, and genders were able to be together as "one body" (3:15; 1 Cor 12:12-27). The formula predated Paul, but he used it because it suited so well his desire to break down the barrier in the church between the Jews ("circumcision," Gen 17:9-14), the original chosen people, and all the rest (see Eph 2:11-18). That also means that all other barriers of privilege and status are abolished in Christ; *all* who have faith—even the barbarous "Scythians"—"are clothed with Christ," are members of the same body.

But, of course, there is tremendous tension here, both for the ancient churches and today. Slavery, for example, continued to be practiced even within the church (3:22-25; Eph 6:5-9; 1 Tim 6:1-2; Titus 2:9-10; 1 Pet 2:18-20)! It took Christianity many more centuries to recognize fully the social

has a grievance against another; as the Lord has forgiven you, so must you also do. [14]And over all these put on love, that is, the bond of perfection. [15]And let the peace of Christ control your hearts, the peace into which you were also called in one body. And be thankful. [16]Let the word of Christ dwell in you richly, as in all wisdom you teach and admonish one another, singing psalms, hymns, and spiritual songs with gratitude in your hearts to God. [17]And whatever you do, in word or in deed, do everything in the name of the Lord Jesus, giving thanks to God the Father through him.

The Christian Family. [18]Wives, be subordinate to your husbands, as is proper in the Lord. [19]Husbands, love your wives, and avoid any bitterness

implications of the gospel. And, truth be told—not least in relation to the full equality of women—the church continues to struggle even today. In any age, what ultimately matters is "Christ," who "is all and *is in all*" (3:11).

As "God's chosen ones," believers must "clothe themselves" with virtues (3:12); this list features qualities of compassion and gentleness, stresses the obligation to forgive "as the Lord forgave you" (3:13; cf. Matt 6:12; 18:21-22), and culminates with "love, the bond of perfection" (3:14). "The peace of Christ" (cf. Phil 4:7) is to "reign in your hearts," and indeed it was into peace "in one body" that believers "were called" (3:15). There is emphasis again on "wisdom" (cf. 2:3) and mutual instruction, but not only in an intellectual sense; "psalms, hymns and spiritual songs" are also to flavor their conversation (3:16). They are to do everything "in the name of the Lord Jesus, giving thanks . . . through him" (3:17).

3:18–4:6 Household rules

Having put "human precepts" in their place (2:22), the writer now provides several precepts as a guide for Christian households. The difference is that these are not offered as essential in themselves; they also, as history has shown, are "shadows" rather than "reality" itself (2:17). This is particularly clear with respect to the instructions to slaves and slave owners. All of these commands presuppose a patriarchal society in which "the master" had legal rights of control and possession with respect to his wife, children, and slaves.

Such "household codes" were quite well known in the ancient world generally and had a considerable impact on the later writings of the New Testament (Eph 5:21–6:9; 1 Pet 2:18–3:7). Particular effort was made to enforce the submission of wives to husbands (Titus 2:5; 1 Cor 14:34-35) and to stop women from being leaders of house-churches (1 Tim 2:11-15).

toward them. ²⁰Children, obey your parents in everything, for this is pleasing to the Lord. ²¹Fathers, do not provoke your children, so they may not become discouraged.

Slaves and Masters. ²²Slaves, obey your human masters in everything, not only when being watched, as currying favor, but in simplicity of heart, fearing the Lord. ²³Whatever you do, do from the heart, as for the Lord and not for others, ²⁴knowing that you will receive from the Lord the due payment of the inheritance; be slaves of the Lord Christ. ²⁵For the wrongdoer will receive recompense for the wrong he committed, and there is no partiality.

4 ¹Masters, treat your slaves justly and fairly, realizing that you too have a Master in heaven.

That women were such leaders is beyond question (e.g., Rom 16:1-15: note Phoebe, Prisca, and Junia; Phil 4:2-3).

The first command here is specifically to "wives" (3:18), not women in general. Single women and widows, particularly if they were wealthy (e.g., Lydia, Acts 16:14), could operate reasonably independently and themselves be heads of households (e.g., Nympha, 4:15). Nowadays husbands and wives properly are "subject to one another" (Eph 5:21, cf. 1 Cor 7:2-5), should "love" and "not be bitter" toward one another, and mothers as well as "fathers" should not "provoke" or "embitter" their children. The command to "obey parents" (3:20) derives from Exodus 20:12 (cf. Mark 10:19).

Most problematic is the command to "slaves" to "obey your human masters in everything" (3:22). Slave owners made full use of such texts to insist that slavery was a divinely ordained institution. Needless to say, this is a "human command" that has thankfully been destroyed (cf. 2:22). The instructions for slaves are lengthier, probably because there were slaves among the letter's recipients—Onesimus, one of those who delivered the letter (4:9), was a slave (Phlm 10-16). Further, Christian faith was already beginning to expose slavery as morally questionable (3:11!) and provided some opportunity for slaves to attain freedom (1 Cor 7:21); 1 Timothy 6:1-2 shows that bitterness could arise between slaves and their Christian masters. The church, however, had no power (yet!) to alter the economic structure of the Roman Empire; it had to conform in order to be accepted (4:5; cf. 1 Tim 6:1; Titus 2:5). The command to "masters" to treat their slaves "justly and fairly" (4:1) was intended to eliminate cruelty, at least among Christian "masters" (cf. 1 Pet 2:18-20).

The remaining exhortations turn first to the theme of constant, thank-filled prayer (4:2; cf. 1 Thess 5:17-18) and include the request that the Colossians should "pray also for us." Once again (as in 1:24-29) Paul and

◄   **Prayer and Apostolic Spirit.** ²Persevere in prayer, being watchful in it with
◄ thanksgiving; ³at the same time, pray for us, too, that God may open a door to us for the word, to speak of the mystery of Christ, for which I am in prison, ⁴that I may make it clear, as I must speak. ⁵Conduct yourselves wisely toward outsiders, making the most of the opportunity. ⁶Let your speech always be gracious, seasoned with salt, so that you know how you should respond to each one.

V. Conclusion

Tychicus and Onesimus. ⁷Tychicus, my beloved brother, trustworthy minister, and fellow slave in the Lord, will tell you all the news of me. ⁸I am sending him to you for this very purpose, so

---

his co-workers are closely associated in the task of proclaiming "the mystery of Christ," for which Paul suffered imprisonment (4:3) and for which he had primary responsibility (4:4; cf. Eph 3:1-7). The command "Conduct yourselves wisely toward outsiders" shows that the church was already becoming a sufficiently public entity that its reputation was important. "Making the most of the opportunity" (or "time") has in mind that time is short before the end (1 Cor 7:29-31). The relationship with outsiders is especially in mind in the final words of instruction; "gracious speech, seasoned with salt" means conversation with others that is wise, good-humored, and interesting. Believers are not to be insipid and boring and certainly not closed off from the world. They must be able rather "to respond to each one," particularly with respect to faith (1 Pet 3:15).

4:7-18 Commendation of co-workers and final greetings

This section seems to require accepting the letter to the Colossians as Paul's own composition, since it is so detailed and personal. Most of the names here also appear in Philemon 23-24. But if such details were enough to make a text original to Paul, then 2 Timothy and Titus would also be his compositions, but very few scholars think that they are. These greetings and commendations make sense when we remember that Paul's mission had always been a team effort. The persons named were part of that team, at least for a short time. If the team—what scholars call "the Pauline school"—and individuals within it were to continue Paul's ministry, they had to assume the authority he exercised and continue the mission in his name. This section says what the writer believes Paul would have said if he could personally greet the Colossians and commend his co-workers to them. The more personal notes regarding Mark (4:10) and Archippus (4:17) deal with real people in real circumstances but do not require Paul himself as author.

that you may know about us and that he may encourage your hearts, ⁹together with Onesimus, a trustworthy and beloved brother, who is one of you. They will tell you about everything here.

From Paul's Co-Workers. ¹⁰Aristarchus, my fellow prisoner, sends you greetings, as does Mark the cousin of Barnabas (concerning whom you have received instructions; if he comes to you, receive him), ¹¹and Jesus, who is called Justus, who are of the circumcision; these alone are my co-workers for the kingdom of God, and they have been a comfort to me. ¹²Epaphras sends you greetings; he is one of you, a slave of Christ [Jesus], always striving for you in his prayers so that you may be perfect and fully assured in all the will

---

Tychicus seems to have joined the team late (Acts 20:4; 2 Tim 4:12; Titus 3:12). He not only brought news of Paul but was also "to encourage [the Colossians'] hearts" (4:8), corresponding exactly to a description of Paul's ministry (2:2). Tychicus carried the letter and would also read it to the gathered community. Onesimus (Phlm 10) was to accompany him; he was from Colossae or thereabouts (4:9). If Colossians was written while Paul was alive, as some think, then it was delivered when Onesimus returned to Philemon.

Aristarchus was from Thessalonica, had traveled with Paul, and had been in prison with him (Acts 19:29; 20:4). "Mark, cousin of Barnabas," accompanied Paul and his cousin during early missions (Acts 12:12; 13:5, 13) and was the cause of a disagreement between Paul and Barnabas (Acts 15:37-39). Barnabas (Acts 4:36-37) was the one who brought Paul into the circle of the apostles (Acts 9:26-27) and was Paul's major companion in the early days (11:29-30; 13:1–15:38), but they had a serious disagreement when Barnabas sided with Peter in Antioch (Gal 2:11-14), and they went their separate ways. This verse (4:10) suggests reconciliation with Mark. "Jesus [a common Jewish name in those days], known as Justus," along with Mark, was "of the circumcision" (i.e., were Jews); they—Mark and Justus—were the "only" Jews who worked with Paul "for the kingdom of God." They were "a comfort" (4:11) in that Paul suffered great distress at the resistance to the gospel among Jews generally (see Rom 9:1-4; 10:1). Other "Jews" had worked with Paul (e.g., Prisca and Aquila, Acts 18:2; Rom 16:3-5); the writer must mean that these were the Jews presently in "the Pauline school." Mention of them supports the letter's point that the Colossians need add no Jewish observances to their life in Christ.

Epaphras was a key figure for the Colossians (1:7). Like Onesimus, he was from Colossae. The description of him as "a slave of Christ" (cf. Rom 1:1; Phil 1:1), "striving for you in his prayers" (4:12) and bearing "much

of God. ¹³For I can testify that he works very hard for you and for those in Laodicea and those in Hierapolis. ¹⁴Luke the beloved physician sends greetings, as does Demas.

A Message for the Laodiceans. ¹⁵Give greetings to the brothers in Laodicea and to Nympha and to the church in her house. ¹⁶And when this letter is read before you, have it read also in the church of the Laodiceans, and you yourselves read the one from Laodicea. ¹⁷And tell Archippus, "See that you fulfill the ministry that you received in the Lord."

¹⁸The greeting is in my own hand, Paul's. Remember my chains. Grace be with you.

---

labor" (the word also denotes "distress") amounts to a very strong commendation (4:13). "Luke, the beloved physician" (2 Tim 4:11; Phlm 24) and "Demas" round off the group sending greetings. There is a later tradition that "Demas deserted" Paul (2 Tim 4:10). Finally, greetings are also sent to "the believers in Laodicea" and to "Nympha and the church in her house" (4:15). Later copiers of the letter changed the text to read "Nymphas and the church in *his* house," since they could not accept that a woman was apparently named as the leader of a church. She probably functioned in a manner similar to Phoebe (Rom 16:1), Stephanas, and others (1 Cor 16:15-18; 1 Thess 5:12-13), that is, as leader of a house-church. "Church" here denotes a small congregation (twenty to forty people?), whereas in 1:18 it means "the church universal."

There is a final command that there must be a sharing of letters. The letter to the Colossians is to be read in Laodicea, the Laodicean letter (presumably from Paul) in Colossae (4:16). The letter to the Laodiceans, of course, is unknown, though there is an apocryphal letter of that name (easily found on the Web). Some think that the letter to the Laodiceans is actually Ephesians or the text on which Ephesians is based. Archippus (4:17) was perhaps Philemon's son (Phlm 2) or, at any rate, was a member of that house-church. In Philemon 2 he is described as Paul's "fellow soldier," but he may have shown some unwillingness to "fulfill the ministry which he received" (4:17).

The greeting in "my [Paul's] own hand" (cf. 1 Cor 16:21; Gal 6:11) assures the readers that the letter is genuinely "from Paul," at least in the sense that it represents well what he would say in these circumstances. The reminder of his imprisonment secures an emotional bond with the recipients. The closing blessing is extremely brief; later copiers added "Amen."

The Letter to the Ephesians

Authorship and destination

Ephesus, on the west coast of Asia Minor (Turkey), was in Paul's day a large seaport city. Paul stayed there for about three years (Acts 20:31) and undoubtedly wrote some of his letters from there, but whether he wrote the letter to the Ephesians is a matter of some doubt.

Ever since the sixteenth century, scholars reading Ephesians in Greek have wondered whether Paul could be its author. Even reading the text in English, those familiar with Paul's letters find reasons to wonder: its ornate, elevated style (especially in chapters 1–3), its purely universal view of "the church," the focus on Christ's cosmic victory over "the powers" with little stress on Christ's death, the comparative lack of apocalyptic expectation combined with a view of salvation already accomplished, the absence of "brothers" as a form of address and of any personal expressions of affection, and the obvious dependence on Colossians—all give reason to question whether Paul is the author. The evidence against Paul as the author is so strong that today about 75 percent of scholars regard Ephesians as pseudonymous.

As with Colossians, however, the issue of authorship may be more complicated. Some, who accept that Paul did not write Colossians, think nevertheless that he may have had some input into that letter. Similarly, with respect to Ephesians, it is possible that the author knew Paul personally—he or she certainly knew Paul's letters (not only Colossians)—or may have written Ephesians expanding on a text written by Paul himself. That text might simply have been Colossians, but a further theory is that Ephesians is an enlarged version of the letter to Laodicea (see Col 4:16). On balance, however, the evidence favors more distance between Paul and Ephesians than these latter theories allow, especially given that Colossians also was probably not composed by the apostle himself.

This commentary will presuppose that Ephesians was written by an admirer of Paul, about twenty or thirty years after his death (i.e., A.D. 80–90). The writer knew Colossians very well, but was also well acquainted with Paul's other letters. Whether Ephesians was originally addressed to Ephesus is doubtful, since first, the words "in Ephesus" (1:1) are missing from the best and earliest manuscripts of the letter, and second, both 1:15 and 3:2 suggest that Paul and the readers had only "heard" of one another, as though Paul had never been there. Whereas Paul's letters always speak to the *particular* circumstances of individual churches, providing specific instructions, Ephesians envisions Paul writing from prison (3:1; 4:1) in *general* terms about challenges for "the church" at large. Ephesians, therefore, is often viewed as a kind of encyclical letter to Paul's churches in general, in Ephesus and elsewhere.

The relationship with Colossians and the purposes of Ephesians

The closeness between Colossians and Ephesians is far more obvious than is the similarity between any other two Pauline letters. This is not to say that they were written by the same author; they probably were not. More probably, the writer of Ephesians composed freely, with major ideas and phrases of Colossians making their presence felt naturally. Some obvious similarities are noted in the commentary on 4:17–5:20. Other passages where similarities are easily detected include:

Ephesians	Colossians	Topic
1:7	1:14	redemption—forgiveness
1:21-23	1:16-19	Christ's victory as head—fullness of God
2:5	2:13	dead made alive
3:2-3	1:25-26	hidden mystery revealed to Paul
5:22–6:9	3:18–4:1	Wives, husbands, children, slaves
4:15-16	2:19	Christ the head—body bound together
6:21-22	4:7-8	Tychicus, the news-bearer

Major themes of Ephesians, most notably the cosmic Christ as head of the universal church, were evidently largely inspired by Colossians; the connection is beyond dispute.

On the other hand, Ephesians is quite different from Colossians in what it says about Judaism. Colossians contests "the philosophy" (Col 2:8), evidently deriving mainly from Judaism, that required obedience to certain laws (2:16-23). Such laws, says Colossians, are mere "human tradition" (2:8, 22), having to do with "the elements of the world" (2:8, 20), which Christ has defeated (2:14-15, 20). Judaism is not specifically mentioned in Colossians, but these warnings portray the Jewish law in a rather negative light; only 3:11 ("no longer Greek and Jew") suggests the possibility of Jewish and Gentile believers living peacefully within the one body.

Ephesians 2:11-18, on the other hand, presumes a very high estimation of Judaism; theirs are "the covenants," to which Gentiles are joined by faith in Christ. The language of "those far off" being brought "near" is Jewish terminology for conversion to Judaism. Most significant is the triple mention of Christ's achieving "peace" (2:14, 15, 17), reconciling Jews and Gentiles "in one body" (2:15-16). It has, therefore, been suggested that Ephesians was written, in part, to reach out to Jewish Christians and present to them a friendly understanding of Paul, softening some of his harshness (e.g., Gal 3:1-21). At the same time, it appeals to Gentile believers to be welcoming of Jewish Christians. In any event, it is clear that Ephesians has a keen concern for the unity of all believers under "one faith" (4:1-6). The primary purpose for its composition, therefore, was to provide a vision of Christ and of "the church" that would make unity among "the churches" and their various believers possible.

The value of Ephesians today

The author of Ephesians lived in a time of transition. The foundational "apostles and prophets" (2:20) had all died. The church, therefore, or better "the churches," had to adjust. Ephesians represents a second/third generation voice that reminds the various churches that they are God's "handiwork, created in Christ Jesus" (2:10) and that they must "live worthily" of their "calling" (4:1). As Paul himself had done, so also the Ephesians writer reminds believers of the fundamentals: they belong together as one body in Christ.

The Catholic Church of the twenty-first century has its own transitions and tensions: What and who is "the church"? How is it to fulfill its mission? Who is to be included in deciding such questions? For all its emphasis on the universal church, Ephesians agrees with the rest of the New Testament that "the church" is the community of the baptized, whether a local congregation (e.g., Col 4:15), "the churches" of a particular region (e.g., Gal 1:2), or the church in general (as in Ephesians). In each manifestation the church is "the body of Christ" (1 Cor 12:27; Eph 1:23), both a physical and a spiritual reality. But in the minds of far too many Catholics, "the church" really only comprises the pope, bishops, and priests; they do not see themselves as truly "the church." Ephesians and the entire New Testament are a corrective to this distortion. Similarly, Ephesians' view of ministry, that it is the task of *all* the baptized (4:11-12), needs to be reaffirmed, as it was by the Second Vatican Council.

Ephesians was written by one of the baptized, a man or woman, perhaps a "teacher," some decades after Paul's death. It represents the voice of the faithful struggling under new and difficult circumstances to recall and remain faithful to the original inspiration of the gospel. The unfathomable "love of Christ" (3:19) is still with the church; Ephesians invites a continuing rediscovery of the ancient tradition so that that love can be more vibrant in the church and so that the church can reach out more effectively to the world.

The Letter to the Ephesians

I. Address

Greeting. ¹Paul, an apostle of Christ Jesus by the will of God, to the holy ones who are [in Ephesus] faithful in Christ Jesus: ²grace to you and peace from God our Father and the Lord Jesus Christ.

The Father's Plan of Salvation. ³Blessed be the God and Father of our Lord Jesus Christ, who has blessed us in Christ with every spiritual blessing in the heavens, ⁴as he chose us in him, before the foundation of the world, to be holy and without blemish before him. In love ⁵he destined us for adoption to himself through Jesus Christ, in accord with the favor of his will, ⁶for the praise of the glory of his grace that he granted us in the beloved.

Fulfillment through Christ. ⁷In him we have redemption by his blood, the forgiveness of transgressions, in accord

1:1-2 Greeting

The opening is very similar to that of 1 Corinthians and nearly identical with that of Colossians. Except for Galatians, Paul's letters always describe believers as "holy," but Ephesians refers to believers as "holy" nine times (e.g., 1:4, 18; 3:8, cf. 2:21; 4:24), proportionally more frequently than any other letter; this accords with the letter's strong ethical emphasis (4:1–6:9). The greeting (1:2) is identical with the longer greeting of Paul's own letters (e.g., Rom 1:7), "grace" being an especially important theological term (see 2:5-8).

1:3-14 A blessing prayer

After the opening, most of Paul's letters have a "thanksgiving," but Ephesians (also 2 Cor 1:3) first has a traditional opening of Jewish prayer, "Blessed be God . . ." (1:3), and then also, quite uniquely, a "thanksgiving" (1:16). Both give thanks by recalling the actions and gifts of God. This "blessing" uses liturgical language; much of its phrasing is hymnlike. There are lots of repetitions: "in Christ" ("in him") occurs nine times, ten times if we include "in the beloved" (1:6); the phrase "for the praise of his glory" occurs three times (1:6, 12, 14). The section comprises a single

▶ This symbol indicates a cross reference number in the *Catechism of the Catholic Church*. See page 123 for number citations.

95

with the riches of his grace [8]that he lavished upon us. In all wisdom and insight, [9]he has made known to us the mystery of his will in accord with his favor that he set forth in him [10]as a plan for the fullness of times, to sum up all things in Christ, in heaven and on earth.

Inheritance through the Spirit. [11]In him we were also chosen, destined in accord with the purpose of the One who accomplishes all things according to the intention of his will, [12]so that we might exist for the praise of his glory,

we who first hoped in Christ. [13]In him you also, who have heard the word of truth, the gospel of your salvation, and have believed in him, were sealed with the promised holy Spirit, [14]which is the first installment of our inheritance toward redemption as God's possession, to the praise of his glory.

II. Unity of the Church in Christ

The Church as Christ's Body. [15]Therefore, I, too, hearing of your faith in the Lord Jesus and of your love for

---

sentence in Greek and features the sort of effusive language that is also found in Colossians (e.g., Col 1:9-20) but is even more prominent here. Phrases like "blessed us with every spiritual blessing" (1:3), "favor of his will" (1:5), "intention of his will" (1:11), and synonymous verbs (e.g., "chose," 1:4; "destined" 1:5, 11) combine to emphasize the abundance of God's favors.

The theological perspective, taking off from Colossians, emphasizes the initiative of God (2:5-10) which in Christ and beyond human calculation "chose" believers "before the foundation of the world" for holiness (1:4; 2:21), "adoption" (1:5), and "redemption" (1:7, 14; Col 1:14). God had always planned for "the gospel of salvation" (1:13); "the mystery of God's will" was "made known" to the faithful (cf. 3:5; Col 1:26), and it was "set forth" (accomplished) in Christ (1:9). God's "plan" and "purpose" were "to sum up all things in Christ" (1:10-11), that is, "to bring all things under Christ as head" (cf. 1:20-22; 4:15), a further key theme taken from Colossians (1:20-22; 4:15, cf. Col 1:18; 2:10).

God's purpose that believers be "holy and blameless" (1:4) consumes the entire second half of the letter (4:1–6:17). But, in a sense, God's purpose has *already* been fulfilled; believers *have* redemption [and] the forgiveness of sins" (1:7; Col 1:14). And yet, for all the emphasis on the *present fulfillment* of blessings, there remains an echo of Paul's point (Rom 8:23; 2 Cor 1:22; 5:5) that the "the holy Spirit" is "the first installment" of coming redemption, not yet its completion (1:14; cf. 4:30).

1:15-23 A thanksgiving prayer

Whereas the "blessing" focuses on what God has accomplished in Christ, this "thanksgiving" is more a prayer that believers will appropriate

Open theater at Ephesus looking down Harbor Road

all the holy ones, [16]do not cease giving thanks for you, remembering you in my prayers, [17]that the God of our Lord Jesus Christ, the Father of glory, may give you a spirit of wisdom and revelation resulting in knowledge of him. [18]May the eyes of [your] hearts be enlightened, that you may know what is the hope that belongs to his call, what are the riches of glory in his inheritance among the holy ones, [19]and what is the surpassing greatness of his power for us who believe, in accord with the exercise of his great might, [20]which he worked in Christ, raising him from the dead and seating him at his right hand in the heavens, [21]far above every principality, authority, power, and dominion,

---

the gifts they have received. If the letter was addressed to Ephesus, then Paul himself could hardly be the author of the opening sentence (*"hearing of your faith"*; also 3:2), since he spent about three years in the city (Acts 20:31). The prayerful thanks, however, are no less sincere, as also the prayer that God will grant them "a spirit of wisdom and revelation by knowledge" of God (1:17). As in Colossians 1:9-10, this prayer highlights the importance of sound knowledge, but here also it is not intellectual knowledge that is primary, but rather deep spiritual recognition, with "the eyes of the heart" (1:18, cf. 3:18-19).

Among the prophets, "knowing God" was the key to the covenant (e.g., Hos 6:6; Isa 11:2; Jer 31:31-34). Here "knowledge" of God involves knowing all the blessings which God has granted in Christ and which this writer delights in listing in heaps of words: "hope," "call," "riches of glory," "inheritance," "the surpassing greatness of God's power" (1:19-20). Believers "know" God's "power," which is at work *now* (in every generation), as it also "worked in Christ," not only "raising him from the dead" but also "seating him" above all powers in the universe (1:20-21). This develops the theme taken over from Colossians (Col 2:15), namely, that Christ's victory, which for Paul would be complete only at the second coming (1 Cor 15:24, cf. Rom 8:38), is complete *now*; God "put all things beneath [Christ's] feet." Dramatic though that is, even more so is the statement that "God gave Christ as head over all things to *the church*" (1:22).

This is the first of nine times that "the church" is mentioned (also 3:10, 21; 5:23-32), and in every instance it refers to the *universal* church, as opposed to a local congregation (e.g., Rom 16:1, 5; Col 4:15). As in Colossians (Col 1:18), the church is a cosmic entity, but this writer expands this idea: as Christ is "head" of the church, so he is the head of all creation (1:10). By virtue of Christ, the church has an extraordinary status and role; according to God's eternal purpose, it is the means by which "God's wisdom is made known" to all the powers of the universe (3:10-11). The church also

and every name that is named not only in this age but also in the one to come. ²²And he put all things beneath his feet and gave him as head over all things to the church, ²³which is his body, the fullness of the one who fills all things in every way.

2 **Generosity of God's Plan.** ¹You were dead in your transgressions and sins ²in which you once lived fol-lowing the age of this world, following the ruler of the power of the air, the spirit that is now at work in the disobedient. ³All of us once lived among them in the desires of our flesh, following the wishes of the flesh and the impulses, and we were by nature children of wrath, like the rest. ⁴But God, who is rich in mercy, because of the great love he had for us, ⁵even when we were

is "seated with [Christ] in the heavens" (2:5-6). To be sure, the writer recognizes that for believers themselves, the victory is not complete (6:10-17). Nevertheless, the vision of a present realization of salvation is extraordinary; Paul's expectation of Christ's imminent return (e.g., 1 Thess 4:13-17) has faded, and suffering is virtually unmentioned (only 3:13; cf. Rom 5:3; Phil 1:29-30). Rather, the church is Christ's (glorified) "body" and his "fullness" within history (1:23; 4:10).

The Greek phrasing of 1:23 is very difficult. The New American Bible translation is possible (see 4:10), but more natural, given the form of the verb, is: "the fullness of the one who *is filled* with respect to all things in every way." As Christ was "raised" and "seated" in heaven (1:20), so also Christ "is filled" with "all the fullness of God" (Col 1:19; 2:9) and will in turn fill believers (3:19; 4:10, 13; Col 2:10). Either way, the vision of the church is breathtaking. Though Christ is head of the universe, only the *church* is Christ's body and fullness. The church, therefore, is the destiny of the universe! Though this is a beautiful spiritual vision, once the church gained power in history, the vision became susceptible to distortion, particularly the notion that all peoples and beliefs must surrender to the church. The church today must be far more humble!

2:1-10 From death to life

The opening phrase (also 2:5) is strongly reminiscent of Colossians 2:13. "The age of this world" and "the ruler of the power of the air" (2:2) presuppose (as does Colossians) that "this world" is dominated by spiritual forces which are beyond human control but which Christ has defeated (Col 2:15). Those evil powers account for the "disobedience" of nonbelievers (2:2), and "all of *us*"—strongly emphasized in the Greek—were once like them and were destined for "wrath" (2:3, cf. 1 Thess 1:10). But God's "great love" seized the initiative and "brought us to life with

dead in our transgressions, brought us to life with Christ (by grace you have been saved), ⁶raised us up with him, and seated us with him in the heavens in Christ Jesus, ⁷that in the ages to come he might show the immeasurable riches of his grace in his kindness to us in Christ Jesus. ⁸For by grace you have been saved through faith, and this is not from you; it is the gift of God; ⁹it is not from works, so no one may boast. ¹⁰For we are his handiwork, created in Christ Jesus for the good works that God has prepared in advance, that we should live in them.

One in Christ. ¹¹Therefore, remember that at one time you, Gentiles in the flesh, called the uncircumcision by those called the circumcision, which is done in the flesh by human hands,

---

Christ" (2:4-5) and "seated us with him in the heavens" (2:6). God's cosmic victory in Christ means that "the coming ages"—perhaps spiritual forces, not just time periods—will see "the richness of [God's] grace" to believers (2:7), who have their home in the heavens (cf. Col 3:3-4).

The writer is at pains to emphasize that God's action was a matter of grace, not of human deserving (cf. Rom 3:27; 4:4-5; Gal 2:16-19). What Paul had said in the context of a debate over Jewish law, this writer applies to "works" in general, so that there will be no "boasting." Paul would agree with the sentiment (e.g., Rom 3:27–4:5); faith itself and the living of it have to do with God's power (Gal 3:23-25; Phil 1:29; 2:13). The point is *not* that humans have no responsibility (Phil 2:12; Gal 5:13–6:10), but simply that neither law nor human action defines the relationship with God (Gal 3:1-14; Eph 2:15; Col 2:14). Believers, as believers, are God's "handiwork." God even "prepared" our "good deeds" in advance! What could emphasize the point more?

2:11-22 The one people of God

As believers had once been "dead in sins," so also they had once been "distant" from the chosen people. There is a switch in this section from God to Christ as the primary actor. The writer displays a high regard for Israel and seems oblivious to any hostility with Jews or the problem of Jews rejecting the gospel. All of this contrasts markedly with Paul's own situation (cf. 1 Thess 2:14-16; 2 Cor 11:24; Rom 9:1-3; 10:1). But this writer says simply that God has "made the two into one new humanity, creating peace" (2:15), as though there was no division between "circumcision" and "uncircumcision" (2:11).

In being "without Christ" Gentiles, as Gentiles, had also been "alienated" from Israel and its "covenants of promise" and therefore were "without hope" (2:12). The writer shares with Paul that, by God's design,

¹²were at that time without Christ, alienated from the community of Israel and strangers to the covenants of promise, without hope and without God in the world. ¹³But now in Christ Jesus you who once were far off have become near by the blood of Christ.

¹⁴For he is our peace, he who made both one and broke down the dividing wall of enmity, through his flesh, ¹⁵abolishing the law with its commandments and legal claims, that he might create in himself one new person in place of the two, thus establishing peace, ¹⁶and might reconcile both with God, in one body, through the cross, putting that enmity to death by it. ¹⁷He came and preached peace to you who were far off and peace to those who were near, ¹⁸for through him we both have access in one Spirit to the Father.

¹⁹So then you are no longer strangers and sojourners, but you are fellow citizens with the holy ones and members

---

Israel, Christ, and the church are intimately connected (cf. Rom 9:1-4; 11:21-31). "But now," "by the blood of Christ" Gentiles have the blessings of Israel. This passage (2:13-16; cf. 1:7) is the closest this letter comes to sustained reflection on the sacrificial death of Jesus; for Paul himself, "Christ crucified" was always the starting-point (e.g., Rom 3:24-26; 1 Cor 1:17–2:2; Gal 3:1-3).

In any event, Christ remains the key. The blessings of Israel are the prize, but the means is Christ, not the law (2:14-15). This is the point of division from Judaism, which believers must recognize while retaining the deepest respect for Judaism and the law, as Paul did (Rom 7:12). Ephesians is implicitly appealing for unity between Jewish and Gentile Christians.

The text again becomes reminiscent of Colossians in seeing Christ's death as destroying "the dividing wall" (2:14), "the law with its . . . legal claims" (2:15; cf. Col 2:14). It is *different*, however, in that here there is no debate with some "philosophy" insisting on laws (cf. Col 2:16-23). This writer sees "the two," Jews and Gentiles, reconciled "to God in one body" (2:16). "In one body" is best understood, in the context, as a reference to the church and perhaps reflects the thought of Colossians, and of Paul himself, that in Christ "there is no longer Greek [Gentile] and Jew" (Col 3:11; Gal 3:28). In other words, the writer is dwelling on the reality of Jews and Gentiles within the church, not on the external relationship of the church with Judaism. Christ "destroyed enmity" and "preached peace" to both Jews and Gentiles (2:17), and "through Christ" all have "access" to God (2:18).

The conclusion is that enmity has been destroyed, at least within the church. All believers, whether Jews or Gentiles, belong to God's household

of the household of God, [20]built upon the foundation of the apostles and prophets, with Christ Jesus himself as the capstone. [21]Through him the whole structure is held together and grows into a temple sacred in the Lord; [22]in him you also are being built together into a dwelling place of God in the Spirit.

III. World Mission of the Church

3 Commission to Preach God's Plan. [1]Because of this, I, Paul, a prisoner of Christ [Jesus] for you Gentiles—[2]if, as I suppose, you have heard of the stewardship of God's grace that was given to me for your benefit, [3][namely, that] the mystery was made known to me by revelation, as I have written

(2:19); reconciliation with God means reconciliation with one another. The writer images the church as an organic, not a static, building; the whole is "jointed together" and "is growing" into a "holy temple" (2:21). This latter phrase would have a particular poignancy, especially for Jews, in light of the destruction of the Jerusalem temple by the Romans in A.D. 70.

The image of the "apostles and prophets" (2:20) as the church's foundation contrasts with Paul's image of "Jesus Christ" as the church's sole foundation (1 Cor 3:11). Ephesians seems deliberately to recall and to nuance Paul's idea. The church is in a new situation: the foundational generation has died, and the church, no longer expecting Christ's imminent return, must look to how it will endure through history. Christ remains "the capstone" (or "keystone") of the building (2:21). In remaining faithful to the "apostles and prophets," the church remains "apostolic" (and prophetic), as it is also "one, holy, and catholic" (universal). All the baptized together are God's "one building in the Spirit" (2:22).

3:1-13 Remembering Paul's ministry

Though not a member of the Twelve, Paul was by far the most important of the apostles within the New Testament (Acts 13–28!), but there were many other "apostles and prophets," men and women alike, who had "labored together in the gospel" (Phil 4:2-3; cf. Rom 16:1-15). But the writer now remembers Paul as the apostle par excellence "for you the Gentiles" (3:1); he had been a prisoner and suffered many times "on your behalf" (also 3:13; 2 Cor 11:21-33). Paul was God's reliable instrument; he had received "God's grace" (3:2, 7; Rom 15:15; Gal 2:9) "for your benefit" (3:2), and "the mystery of Christ" "by revelation" (3:3-4, cf. Gal 1:11-12). The writer knew Paul's letters (not only Colossians), and believers could "read" them (not only Ephesians) "to understand [Paul's] insight" (3:4) for themselves.

briefly earlier. [4]When you read this you can understand my insight into the mystery of Christ, [5]which was not made known to human beings in other generations as it has now been revealed to his holy apostles and prophets by the Spirit, [6]that the Gentiles are coheirs, members of the same body, and co-partners in the promise in Christ Jesus through the gospel.

[7]Of this I became a minister by the gift of God's grace that was granted me in accord with the exercise of his power. [8]To me, the very least of all the holy ones, this grace was given, to preach to the Gentiles the inscrutable riches of Christ, [9]and to bring to light [for all] what is the plan of the mystery hidden from ages past in God who created all things, [10]so that the manifold wisdom of God might now be made known through the church to the principalities and authorities in the heavens. [11]This was according to the eternal purpose

This passage (3:2-7) recalls and develops Colossians 1:25-27. It presupposes, in the manner of apocalyptic literature (e.g., Dan 8:17-19), that God's plan of salvation is ancient, but "in other generations" (3:5) had been kept secret until the appointed time (cf. 3:9). In Colossians the recipients of "the mystery" are all the baptized (Col 1:26), but here, consistent with their founding role, the primary recipients are "the holy apostles and prophets" (3:5), that is, Paul himself and those who worked with him. The content of "the mystery" recalls 2:11-18: "the Gentiles," "through the gospel," share in the fulfilled "promise" to Israel. It was this gospel—the inclusion of the Gentiles—for which Paul was commissioned by God's "power" (3:7; cf. Gal 1:16).

For a third time Paul's apostolate is referred to as "the grace given" by God (3:8; cf. 3:2, 7), and again it is emphasized that Paul received this apostolate "to preach to the Gentiles." Why such emphatic repetition was thought necessary is impossible to know. During his ministry Paul had not been accepted by all as an "apostle" (1 Cor 9:1-2; Gal 1:1–2:9) and had conceded that he was "the last of the apostles" (1 Cor 15:9). Here he is referred to as "the least of all the saints" (3:8), which brings into sharp relief how great was God's grace. Paul had highlighted the same contrast in his autobiographical accounts (1 Cor 15:8-10; Gal 1:13-16). He knew from personal experience that God often chooses the most unlikely instrument to advance the gospel (1 Cor 1:27-29).

It is a unique thought that the purpose of Paul's apostolate was so that "God's manifold wisdom might be made known to the heavenly principalities and authorities," those powers that Christ had defeated (1:20-22). Indeed, this had happened "through the church," which means that now

that he accomplished in Christ Jesus our Lord, [12]in whom we have boldness of speech and confidence of access through faith in him. [13]So I ask you not to lose heart over my afflictions for you; this is your glory.

Prayer for the Readers. [14]For this reason I kneel before the Father, [15]from whom every family in heaven and on earth is named, [16]that he may grant you in accord with the riches of his glory to be strengthened with power through his Spirit in the inner self, [17]and that Christ may dwell in your hearts through faith; that you, rooted and grounded in love, [18]may have strength to comprehend with all the holy ones what is the breadth and length and height and depth, [19]and to know the love of Christ that surpasses knowledge, so that you may be filled with all the fullness of God.

[20]Now to him who is able to accomplish far more than all we ask or imagine, by the power at work within us, [21]to him be glory in the church and in

---

the church participates with Christ in the continuing mop-up campaign against "the devil" (6:11-12). "By God's eternal purpose, made effective in Christ" (3:11), the church can be "bold" in this endeavor (3:12) and should not be discouraged at the thought of Paul's "afflictions" (3:13).

3:14-21 A prayer

The intensity of already intense language is now increased as the writer breaks into prayer that God will enable believers to have greater and greater power in the Spirit "to know" the unknowable "love of Christ" (3:19). The prayer has two parts: a petition (3:16-19) and a doxology (3:20-21).

"For this reason" recalls 3:1 and that this is "Paul" at prayer, on his "knees" before "the Father" of the universe. The heart of Christian spirituality is caught in the petition; the "power" derives purely from "the Spirit," but it is not a power for doing (cf. 2:8-9) so much as for *surrendering* "by faith," so that "Christ may well in your hearts" (2:16-17). This is reminiscent of Paul's great claim, "I no longer live, rather Christ lives within me" (Gal 2:20), which he claimed for believers generally, not just himself (cf. Rom 6:8-11). All believers are to "be rooted and founded in love" (cf. Col 1:23; 2:7). This means primarily "the love" that Christ has shown (2:4; cf. Gal 2:20; 1 John 4:10), as the next part of the petition indicates, but believers' love for others (4:2, 15; 5:2) and for "the Lord" (6:24) is also envisioned. Believers do "know" that love, but the prayer asks for their (ongoing) "strengthening" to plumb the unfathomable "love of Christ" in all its dimensions (3:18-19). The end of the journey is "to be filled" by Christ (1:23) "with all the fullness of God" (cf. 4:10-13; Col 1:19; 2:9-10).

Christ Jesus to all generations, forever and ever. Amen.

Unity in the Body. [1]I, then, a prisoner for the Lord, urge you to live in a manner worthy of the call you have received, [2]with all humility and gentleness, with patience, bearing with one another through love, [3]striving to preserve the unity of the spirit through the bond of peace: [4]one body and one Spirit, as you were also called to the one hope of your call; [5]one Lord, one faith, one baptism; [6]one God and Father of all, who is over all and through all and in all.

Diversity of Gifts. [7]But grace was given to each of us according to the measure of Christ's gift. [8]Therefore, it says:

"He ascended on high and took prisoners captive;
he gave gifts to men."

[9]What does "he ascended" mean except that he also descended into the lower [regions] of the earth? [10]The one who

As the petition hints at the cosmic reach of Christ's love, so the doxology praises God, who, as "Father" of the universe (3:15), can (and will) "accomplish far more than all we ask or imagine" and whose "glory" both "in the church" and "in Christ Jesus" exceeds the universe and all the powers within it (3:20-21).

4:1-16 Growing to maturity in Christ

"The church" is not explicitly mentioned in this section, but the focus on "unity" (4:3-6, 13) and "ministry" (4:11-12) as the means for "the whole body" (4:16) to grow to maturity in Christ shows that the church and how it functions are the main concerns. But this is not mere description; rather, the writer proclaims that the church must "live" by these ideals if it is to be true to its "calling" (4:1, 4). Though there is now emphasis on human responsibility, the priority of "grace" (as in 2:8) remains prominent (4:7-11).

The reminder of Paul's being "a prisoner" adds deep feeling to the "appeal" (cf. Rom 12:1) that believers "live in a manner worthy" of their "call" (4:1). The narrative of God's "call" filled the first part of the letter and now leads to the imperative of believers' existence. And the first imperative is to be "humble," "gentle," "patient," and "loving" toward one another; only so will true "unity" be maintained. "Unity" is a gift of "the Spirit," but it can be destroyed; "the bond of peace" is a way of summarizing all the qualities needed to preserve it. Thus "the spirit" in "the unity of the spirit" is both human and divine; even God's gifts sometimes need human cooperation. Unity here and now ("one body") is to mirror "the one hope" (redemption, 1:14) to which believers "were called" (4:4).

descended is also the one who ascended far above all the heavens, that he might fill all things.

[11]And he gave some as apostles, others as prophets, others as evangelists, others as pastors and teachers, [12]to equip the holy ones for the work of ministry, for building up the body of Christ, [13]until we all attain to the unity of faith and knowledge of the Son of God,

---

The early churches were inevitably quite diverse in many respects. There was, for instance, more than one baptismal formula. Matthew's (Matt 28:19) finally became standard, but it is not the same as Paul's (Gal 3:28; cf. 1 Cor 12:13), which itself was not fixed (cf. Col 3:11). Ephesians (4:4-6) reflects a further formula or, at least, additional liturgical language of baptism. The insistence here that there must be "one faith, one baptism" (4:5) bespeaks attempts of the early churches, no matter how diverse or scattered, to be "one body." The emphasis here on God as the "one God" of the entire universe (4:6) furthered these efforts considerably. For the New Testament (e.g., John 17:20-23), Christians being divided among themselves is unthinkable.

The writer now picks up a theme well known in Paul's own writing, namely, that "to each one" in the church God has given some "measure of Christ's gift" (4:7; cf. Rom 12:3-8; 1 Cor 12:4-11). This is reinforced by reference to Psalm 68:19, which, in the context of recounting God's saving deeds for Israel, actually speaks of God's *"receiving* gifts" from Israel's, and God's, enemies. Jewish tradition applied the psalm to *Moses* "ascending" Mount Sinai and receiving gifts from God. Ephesians seems to reflect that idea but switches the text to speak of *Christ's* "ascending" and *"giving* gifts" to the church. As the writer sees it, it was Christ who "ascended on high and took captivity captive," the same victory that was earlier described as *God's* action (1:20-22). Having despoiled the powers, Christ distributed the enemy's wealth, so to speak, to the church (cf. Mark 3:27).

The writer pauses to dwell further on the psalm in relation to Christ: he who "ascended" and "filled" the universe with his presence (4:10) first "descended to the lower regions of the earth" (4:9). This is sometimes interpreted to refer to Christ "descending to the dead" (as in the Apostles' Creed; cf. 1 Pet 3:19), but far more likely, it refers to the incarnation (as in John 3:13).

Christ's gift of "apostles" and "prophets" and other primary ministers (4:11) was bestowed so that the church might be the fully functioning "body of Christ" (4:12, 16). It is perhaps important to emphasize that women, as well as men, were such primary ministers (e.g., Rom 16:1-12;

to mature manhood, to the extent of the full stature of Christ, [14]so that we may no longer be infants, tossed by waves and swept along by every wind of teaching arising from human trickery, from their cunning in the interests of deceitful scheming. [15]Rather, living the truth in love, we should grow in every way into him who is the head, Christ, [16]from whom the whole body, joined and held together by every supporting ligament, with the proper functioning of each part, brings about the body's growth and builds itself up in love.

Phil 4:2-3; Acts 2:17-18; 21:9). Paul had taught that "God designated some in the church to be, first, apostles; second, prophets; third, teachers" (1 Cor 12:28), but that listing followed on his insistence that *every* member of the church had some "spiritual gift" or "ministry" "for the common good" (12:4-7) and that no one's contribution was to be neglected or despised (12:14-27). Both Paul and Ephesians agree that the primary ministers are not to be the only ministers, but are rather "to equip the *holy ones for the work of ministry*" (4:11-12), an emphasis taken up vigorously by the Second Vatican Council, but sometimes, even today, forgotten. The writer adds "the evangelists [and] the pastors" (4:11) to Paul's list, which reflects the new situation of ministry toward the end of the first century. Later "bishop," "presbyter," and "deacon" became established titles (e.g., 1 Tim 3:1-13; Titus 1:5), and, sadly, women were increasingly excluded from leadership (1 Tim 2:11-15).

All gifts and ministries have the same aims (4:13), which, in various ways, have already been named: "building of the body" (2:21-22), "unity of faith" (4:5), maturity and "the fullness of Christ" (1:23; cf. 3:19). The purpose of leadership is then stated in negative terms so that the church will not be tossed about "by every wind of teaching" arising from "human trickery" (4:14). To the contrary, the church is to be characterized by "speaking the truth in love" so as "to grow into Christ, the head, in every way" (4:15; cf. 1:22).

Paul himself had not extended the image of "the body of Christ" (1 Cor 12:27) to Christ being its "head." Later on this notion, especially in combination with 5:23 ("wives subordinate to their husbands"), contributed to a very patriarchal view of the church. As used here, however, it is a beautiful, dynamic notion of the church organically growing toward Christ and his "fullness." The church not only grows into Christ, it also grows from him, as well as from the functioning of all its members, and so "builds itself up in love" (4:16). The key to the whole is the unity of believers with one another and with Christ (4:3-6, 13, 16).

Renewal in Christ. [17]So I declare and testify in the Lord that you must no longer live as the Gentiles do, in the futility of their minds; [18]darkened in understanding, alienated from the life of God because of their ignorance, because of their hardness of heart, [19]they have become callous and have handed themselves over to licentiousness for the practice of every kind of impurity to excess. [20]That is not how you learned Christ, [21]assuming that you have heard of him and were taught in him, as truth is in Jesus, [22]that you should put away the old self of your former way of life, corrupted through deceitful desires, [23]and be renewed in the spirit of your minds, [24]and put on the new self, created in God's way in righteousness and holiness of truth.

4:17–5:20 Once darkness, not light

This very long section of ethical exhortation is, in part, dependent on Colossians but also has some unique concerns and images. The dependence on Colossians is apparent in a long list of words, phrases, and concepts that are sometimes almost identical with the earlier letter. Examples include: "old self"—"new self" (4:22-24; Col 3:9-10); "forgive as God forgave you" (4:32; Col 3:13); "greed" as "idolatry" (5:5; Col 3:5); "wrath" for the "disobedient" (5:6; Col 3:6); "psalms, hymns and songs" (5:19; Col 3:16), and so on. Ephesians is unique, however, in its much stronger use of the imagery of "light" versus "darkness" (4:18; 5:8-9, 11-14, cf. Col 1:12-13), its concern for "anger" and proper speech among believers (e.g., 4:31), and a stronger emphasis on separation from outsiders (5:6-7; cf. Col 4:5-6).

The writer solemnly warns believers ("I testify in the Lord") that they must be different from "the Gentiles." Most readers, though not all, were "Gentiles," in the sense that their natural heritage was not in Judaism (3:1; 2:11); but "Gentiles," even in Paul's time (e.g., 1 Cor 5:1), was used to refer to non-believers, who, unlike Jews and Christians, did not acknowledge the one God (1 Thess 4:5). As the imminent expectation of Christ's return receded and the church, though still a small minority, became a *part of* society, as opposed to watching and waiting for its destruction (see 1 Cor 1:18; 7:29-31), it became increasingly necessary for Christians to distinguish themselves from the dominant culture, although living within it. Baptism and other rituals, as well as "the faith," were essential boundary markers, but on a day-to-day basis even more important was (and is) "living" by the highest ethical ideals.

The writer vividly portrays "Gentile" behavior as "futile" ("foolish"), having no understanding of "the life of God" (the life that God enables) because of "the hardness of their hearts" and their consequent surrender

IV. Daily Conduct, an Expression of Unity

Rules for the New Life. [25]Therefore, putting away falsehood, speak the truth, each one to his neighbor, for we are members one of another. [26]Be angry but do not sin; do not let the sun set on your anger, [27]and do not leave room for the devil. [28]The thief must no longer steal, but rather labor, doing honest work with his [own] hands, so that he may have something to share with one in need. [29]No foul language should come out of your mouths, but only such as is good for needed edification, that it may impart grace to those who hear. [30]And do not grieve the holy Spirit of God, with which you were sealed for

---

of themselves to "every kind of impurity" (4:17-19). Such negative evaluations of "outsiders" by "insiders" inevitably arise among emerging religious groups; they change, however, if a group—as happened with Christianity—itself becomes dominant. Power changes perspectives. Believers today have to be humble in their evaluations of "outsiders" and have to apply to *themselves* Scripture's many warnings about "ignorance" and "excess" (4:18-19).

When believers "learned Christ" (a completely unique expression), the learning had nothing to do with being either "callous" or "impure" (4:19-20), and therefore the transformation from "the old self" to "the new" must mean putting aside "deceitful desires" and turning to "holiness" (4:22-24). The dependence on Colossians 3:8-11 shows that baptism is in mind here. The "new self, created by God's design" (4:24), transforms the relationship with God and with others.

The next paragraph (4:25-32) follows a pattern of mentioning, first, the vice to be avoided and then the good to be espoused. There is clear encouragement for truthful and loving words, as there is also, throughout the letter, a deep concern about "falsehood" (4:14, 22, 25; 5:6) and about the misguided "impulses" (2:3) and "futile thinking" (4:17-18), which impede true knowledge and understanding (e.g., 4:13-14; 5:17-18). The writer quotes Zechariah 8:16 to urge believers to "speak the truth" and adds as motivation, "For we are members of one another" (4:25, cf. Rom 12:5). Psalm 4:5 is quoted to make the point that "anger" (though inevitable) must not become "sin"; "Do not let the sun set on your anger" was proverbial even then. "Anger" here denotes the "fury" that leads to "bitterness" and "shouting" (4:31) and provides "an opportunity for the devil" (4:27; cf. 6:11; 2 Cor 2:11). Far from "stealing," all must "work with their own hands" (cf. 1 Thess 4:11) and be prepared "to share with anyone in need" (4:28).

the day of redemption. [31]All bitterness, fury, anger, shouting, and reviling must be removed from you, along with all malice. [32][And] be kind to one another, compassionate, forgiving one another as God has forgiven you in Christ.

5 [1]So be imitators of God, as beloved children, [2]and live in love, as Christ loved us and handed himself over for us as a sacrificial offering to God for a fragrant aroma. [3]Immorality or any impurity or greed must not even be mentioned among you, as is fitting among holy ones, [4]no obscenity or silly or suggestive talk, which is out of place, but instead, thanksgiving. [5]Be sure of this, that no immoral or impure or greedy person, that is, an idolater, has any inheritance in the kingdom of Christ and of God.

"Foul speech" ought to have no place among believers (5:3-4), but speech must rather be "good" for "building" the church and "imparting grace" (4:29). The injunction not to "grieve the holy Spirit" reflects Isaiah 63:10, which recalls Israel's "provoking God's holy Spirit" by disobedience. The rest of that verse (4:30) repeats the thought of 1:13-14, namely, that by faith believers were "sealed with the holy Spirit" as a "pledge" of the coming "redemption." Meanwhile, destructive anger and the bitter words that accompany it must be "removed" (4:31); in their place belong kindness, compassion, and "forgiving one another" as God has forgiven us (4:32, cf. Col 3:13; Matt 6:14).

To forgive as God forgives leads naturally to the thought that believers become "imitators of God" (cf. Matt 5:48), living like God's "beloved children" (5:1) and like Christ who "loved us" to the point of "surrendering himself for us" as a "sacrifice to God" (5:2). Paul urged his churches to "imitate" himself (e.g., 1 Cor 11:1; Phil 3:17); the exhortation to imitate God is unique to this letter. The following warnings focus especially on sexual morality (actions and speech) and on "greed," which is equated with "idolatry" (5:5; Col 3:5). The repeated warning against "obscenity . . . or suggestive talk" (5:4; cf. 4:29) perhaps indicates that the writer had witnessed or at least heard of such inappropriate speech among the churches. "Thanksgiving" should better characterize their conversation, as well as the awareness that immorality forfeits salvation (5:5).

Perhaps a particular person or teaching is in mind with the warning against "empty arguments." That warning and the explanation that such things bring "the wrath of God on the disobedient" (5:6) closely imitate Colossians (Col 2:8; 3:6), where a particular problem was in view. In any event, the writer wishes for there to be a clear boundary between the church and, at least, the "immoral" ones in society who were alluded to in

The Library of Celsus in Ephesus, which provided space for twelve thousand scrolls

Duty to Live in the Light. ⁶Let no one deceive you with empty arguments, for because of these things the wrath of God is coming upon the disobedient. ⁷So do not be associated with them. ⁸For you were once darkness, but now you are light in the Lord. Live as children of light, ⁹for light produces every kind of goodness and righteousness and truth. ¹⁰Try to learn what is pleasing to the Lord. ¹¹Take no part in the fruitless works of darkness; rather expose them, ¹²for it is shameful even to mention the things done by them in secret; ¹³but everything exposed by the light becomes visible, ¹⁴for everything that becomes visible is light. Therefore, it says:

"Awake, O sleeper,
and arise from the dead,
and Christ will give you light."

¹⁵Watch carefully then how you live, not as foolish persons but as wise,

the previous warnings—"do not be associated with them" (5:7; cf. 5:11). This compares interestingly with Paul's words to the Corinthians, distinguishing between the "immoral of this world," with whom association was unavoidable, and the "immoral" within the church (1 Cor 5:9-13). For Paul, it was the latter that were the real threat.

The contrast this writer draws between the church and the larger society is abundantly apparent in the following verses (5:8-14) with their imagery of "light" and "darkness." Prior to "learning Christ" (4:20), believers were "darkness," but now "in the Lord" they "*are* light" and must "live as children of light," which recalls 5:1: "Be imitators of God." "Light" as a metaphor for God and the realm of God is very common in Scripture (e.g., Ps 27:1; 44:4; Isa 9:2; 60:1, 19-20; Mic 7:8; John 1:4-9; 8:12). The darkness is not beyond God's realm, but it resists God's invitation (cf. John 3:20-21). Light, on the other hand, produces every kind of goodness (5:9), discerns "what is pleasing to the Lord," and "exposes" the "hidden, shameful" deeds of darkness as evil (5:10-12).

The next verses (5:13-14) are difficult, and interpretation has to squeeze out of the text what it does not precisely say. To "be exposed by the light" and thus to "become visible" means to "come into the light," which presumably has something to do with conversion. Indeed, perhaps the writer is suggesting that believers have an obligation so to "expose" and indict as evil "the fruitless works of darkness" (5:11) that evildoers will come to the light of Christ. It is perhaps in that sense that "what [or whoever] becomes visible *is* [or 'becomes'?] light" (5:14) and is identified with Christ. The quotation supports this interpretation, since it is almost certainly a baptism hymn (cf. Rom 6:3-4) and addresses the newly baptized: "Awake, O sleeper, and arise from the dead, and Christ will shine on you" (cf. Isa

◄ ¹⁶making the most of the opportunity,
◄ because the days are evil. ¹⁷Therefore, do not continue in ignorance, but try to understand what is the will of the Lord. ¹⁸And do not get drunk on wine, in which lies debauchery, but be filled
◄ with the Spirit, ¹⁹addressing one another [in] psalms and hymns and spiritual songs, singing and playing to the Lord in your hearts, ²⁰giving thanks ► always and for everything in the name of our Lord Jesus Christ to God the Father.

Wives and Husbands. ²¹Be subordi- ► nate to one another out of reverence for Christ. ²²Wives should be subordinate

---

60:1). Ephesians, of course, intends the reminder for more than just the newly baptized. Ultimately, believers, like Jesus (John 8:12), are to be "the light of the world" (Matt 5:16).

The whole congregation is to see that they "walk" as "wise ones" (5:15), "making the best of the opportunity" (Col 4:5) in the midst of the present "evil days" (5:16; cf. 6:13). Neither being "ignorant" ("foolish") nor "getting drunk" will enable the proper "understanding" that is so essential (4:17-18, cf. 3:18-19; 4:13-14). This long section comes to an end by again borrowing from Colossians (Col 3:16), exhorting believers, "filled with the Spirit" (5:18), to share "psalms and hymns" with one another (such as 5:14) and constantly to "give thanks . . . to God the Father" (5:19-20).

5:21–6:9 Household rules

This section obviously corresponds to, and is a development of, Colossians 3:18–4:1. The development is noteworthy. Ephesians dwells at far greater length on men's obligation to love their wives and, in comparing that love to Christ's love for the church, produces an impressive meditation on the relationship between Christ and the church. Nevertheless, the same enormous problems regarding the "subordination" of wives and the "obedience" of slaves exist for Ephesians as for Colossians. Both presuppose the unquestioned patriarchal structure of first-century society.

Whereas, in other respects, Ephesians wants the church to be different from the rest of society (5:7, 11) and probably sees these instructions also as furthering that purpose, society's template with regard to marriage and slavery remains unchanged. For Ephesians, the "difference" is a greater measure of "love" for wives (5:25) and less "bullying" ("threatening") for slaves (6:9). It has taken until modern times for the *structures* of society and for the church itself to change, and the process is not even yet complete. We cannot, therefore, judge them; we have to turn the eye of discernment onto ourselves, and how we interpret and apply these verses is a test for that discernment.

to their husbands as to the Lord. ²³For the husband is head of his wife just as Christ is head of the church, he himself the savior of the body. ²⁴As the church is subordinate to Christ, so wives should be subordinate to their husbands in everything. ²⁵Husbands, love your wives, even as Christ loved the church and handed himself over for her ²⁶to sanctify her, cleansing her by the bath of water with the word, ²⁷that he might present to himself the church in splendor, without spot or wrinkle or any such thing, that she might be holy and without blemish. ²⁸So [also] husbands should love their wives as their own bodies. He who loves his wife loves himself. ²⁹For no one hates his own flesh but rather nourishes and cherishes it, even as Christ does the church, ³⁰because we are members of his body.

³¹"For this reason a man shall leave
[his] father and [his] mother
and be joined to his wife,
and the two shall become one flesh."

³²This is a great mystery, but I speak in reference to Christ and the church. ³³In any case, each one of you should love his wife as himself, and the wife should respect her husband.

Verse 21, grammatically, could as well be included with the previous section as with this one, but its verb ("be subordinate") is intended to be applied in a special way to "wives" (5:22). The author assumes that wives ought to "subordinate" themselves to their husbands (cf. 1 Pet 3:1-6) and, going beyond Colossians, strengthens this idea by weaving it into the theme of Christ as "the head of the church" (5:23). The *distortion* of this text that sometimes leads women to think they must stay with an abusive husband or men to think they have a right to hit their wives (!) has been criticized strongly by the American Catholic bishops. It intends, in fact, to make Christian marriage into a model of the love Christ has for the church and probably also into a demonstration of the goodness of Christian faith. We can certainly affirm that intention and that spouses should subordinate themselves to *one another* (5:21; 1 Cor 7:4).

The idea that Christ's death was, specifically, "for the sake of" the *church* (5:25) is unique to this letter. Paul's emphasis—the two thoughts are not contradictory—was that Christ died "for the ungodly" (Rom 3:23-26; 5:6-8), outsiders being more clearly included. That sacrifice is to be a model, for wives and husbands alike, of how they are to love one another. Christ "sanctified" the church, "cleansing" it both by his death and by baptism (5:26). The church is imaged here as Christ's bride (cf. Ezek 16:8-9), whom he will espouse to himself at the final judgment "in splendor," "holy and blameless" (5:27).

6 **Children and Parents.** ¹Children, obey your parents [in the Lord], for this is right. ²"Honor your father and mother." This is the first commandment with a promise, ³"that it may go well with you and that you may have a long life on earth." ⁴Fathers, do not provoke your children to anger, but bring them up with the training and instruction of the Lord.

Slaves and Masters. ⁵Slaves, be obedient to your human masters with fear and trembling, in sincerity of heart, as to Christ, ⁶not only when being watched, as currying favor, but as slaves of Christ, doing the will of God from the heart, ⁷willingly serving the Lord and not human beings, ⁸knowing that each will be requited from the Lord for whatever good he does, whether he is slave or free.

To love one's spouse is also to "love oneself" (5:28), one's own "body" and "flesh" (5:29). That, says the writer, was how "Christ loved the church, since we are members of his body" (5:29-30; cf. 1 Cor 12:27). Mention of "flesh" prepares for the quotation from Genesis 2:24, which is the climax of the second creation story (the first = Gen 1:1–2:4). That story focuses primarily on humans and the creation of sex and marriage (Gen 2:20-24). Ephesians takes that text—most notably, "the two shall become one flesh"—and applies it, as "a great mystery . . . to Christ and to the church" (5:31-32) and the "marriage" between them. How ironic and tragic that such a beautiful image has sometimes been a device for violence, including the violence of the subordination of women to men. The writer returns to the theme of marriage in the church and emphasizes that "each man should love his wife as himself" and, as ancient society would expect, that "the wife should respect [literally 'fear'] her husband" (5:33). *Mutual love* and respect would properly be our modern emphasis.

The command that children should "obey" their parents (6:1) is nearly identical with Colossians 3:20 but adds motivation by quoting Deuteronomy 5:16 (cf. Exod 20:12). Different words (from Colossians) are used to instruct "fathers"—we would say "parents"—not to "provoke children to anger" (6:3). The command to "raise children in the instruction of the Lord" (6:4) is unique to Ephesians. The lengthy instructions to "slaves" (6:5-8), as in Colossians 3:22-25, probably indicate both the presence of slaves among the readers and the need to make slavery compatible with faith. "There is no longer slave nor free" (Gal 3:28) is being compromised. As the husband is likened to Christ (5:23), so also is the slave master (6:5), with terrible effects in later history. We can apply to ourselves the exhortations to serve "in sincerity of heart," rather than for "currying favor"

⁹Masters, act in the same way towards them, and stop bullying, knowing that both they and you have a Master in heaven and that with him there is no partiality.

Battle against Evil. ¹⁰Finally, draw your strength from the Lord and from his mighty power. ¹¹Put on the armor of God so that you may be able to stand firm against the tactics of the devil. ¹²For our struggle is not with flesh and blood but with the principalities, with the powers, with the world rulers of this present darkness, with the evil spirits in the heavens. ¹³Therefore, put on the armor of God, that you may be able to resist on the evil day and, having done everything, to hold your ground. ¹⁴So stand fast with your loins girded in truth, clothed with righteousness as a breastplate, ¹⁵and your feet shod in readiness for the gospel of peace. ¹⁶In all circumstances, hold faith as a shield, to quench all [the] flaming

---

(6:5-6), and fruitfully be aware that there is one God "in heaven" over all, no matter status or identity (6:8-9).

6:10-20 Final exhortations

In this final section the writer envisions Christian life as a great battle against "the evil spiritual powers" (6:12) that Christ has defeated (1:20-22). The battle continues because believers *are* "flesh and blood," but the evil they battle is not (6:12). Ultimately, in spite of 2:4-8, even Ephesians knows that the process of salvation is not yet complete. Therefore, especially through prayer (6:18-20), believers need *God's* "strength" and "armor" to withstand "the tactics of the devil" (6:11-13). "The evil day" (6:13) is the time of "temptation" ("testing") and "evil," from which we also pray to be delivered in the Lord's Prayer (Matt 6:13).

Drawing on Old Testament texts listing the weaponry of God (Isa 11:5; 59:16-17; Wis 5:16-23), the writer describes the (primarily defensive) armor that will see believers through the fight: "the girdle of truth," "the breastplate of righteousness," and so on (6:14-17). "The gospel of peace" (6:15) might better be translated "the *proclamation* of peace," meaning that believers must be "ready" to witness to the "peace" that God gives and thereby to "extinguish the flaming arrows" aimed at them (6:16). This passage, in other words (cf. 5:11-14), might be a hint of some concern for defense of the gospel among non-believers. The only *offensive* weapon in the believer's armor is "the sword of the Spirit, which is the word of God" (6:17); evangelization, that is, sharing the gospel, is part of the believer's task. "The word" is not to be identified with the Bible or any part of it; "the word" is "alive and active" (Heb 4:12) in and among believers. The Bible enables us to recognize "the word," but it does not define it.

arrows of the evil one. [17]And take the helmet of salvation and the sword of the Spirit, which is the word of God.

Constant Prayer. [18]With all prayer and supplication, pray at every opportunity in the Spirit. To that end, be watchful with all perseverance and supplication for all the holy ones [19]and also for me, that speech may be given me to open my mouth, to make known with boldness the mystery of the gospel [20]for which I am an ambassador in chains, so that I may have the courage to speak as I must.

V. Conclusion

A Final Message. [21]So that you also may have news of me and of what I am doing, Tychicus, my beloved brother and trustworthy minister in the Lord, will tell you everything. [22]I am sending him to you for this very purpose, so that you may know about us and that he may encourage your hearts.

[23]Peace be to the brothers, and love with faith, from God the Father and the Lord Jesus Christ. [24]Grace be with all who love our Lord Jesus Christ in immortality.

It is for continued, vigorous sharing of "the mystery of the gospel" (6:19) that the writer asks the recipients to pray, as they also pray for themselves and "for all the holy ones" (6:18), that is, the church. The final reminder of Paul's "imprisonment" keeps the great apostle's memory present as the letter draws to a close (6:20).

6:21-24 Conclusion

The note about Tychicus's bringing "news" of Paul and "that he may encourage your hearts" (6:21-22) is nearly word-for-word identical with Colossians 4:7-8. The letter concludes, wishing "peace to believers." "Love with faith" (6:23) is unique to Ephesians, as is the final blessing. On the other hand, "grace" was a key term in Paul's theology (e.g., Rom 3:24; 11:6, cf. Eph 2:8) and in all his final blessings. Paul and Ephesians agree: "grace" is the beginning and the end of Christian existence, and our only hope for "immortality" (6:24). Many manuscripts add "Amen."

REVIEW AIDS AND DISCUSSION TOPICS

I Thessalonians

1. What are the primary sources for understanding Paul? Why are the letters more important than Acts in this regard? Which letters were certainly written by Paul himself? (pp. 5, 9–11)

2. Why did Paul write 1 Thessalonians and what is its value for the Church today? What were Paul's feelings for the Thessalonians? (pp. 11–13, 20–21)

3. Describe "the Church of the Thessalonians": How many people? Was there more than one "church"? What did their conversion to Jesus involve? (pp. 15–16)

4. Religion and money-grubbing often go together. How does the letter indicate Paul's concern not to be seen as corrupt? (pp. 17–18)

5. How do you feel about Paul's language in 2:14-16? How do you think we should interpret such words today? (pp. 19–20)

6. In almost every generation some have claimed that "these are the last days." How do you respond to Christians who claim that "*these* are the last days" and that "outside of the Christian faith there is no salvation"? (pp. 25–27)

7. To whom does the task of ministry belong? Could women be leaders? If leaders make mistakes, what is the Church to do? (pp. 28–29)

Philippians

1. There are many facets to this letter? What do you like most about it?

2. Why was Philippi a notable city and how does Paul show awareness of its importance? What was its importance to Paul, particularly in terms of support for his ministry? (pp. 31, 34, 51–52)

3. What do you think of Paul's attitude in the face of opposition, imprisonment and possible death? Is he a starry-eyed optimist in need of a reality-check? (pp. 35–39, 44)

4. What does it mean to say that "faith is a gift" (p. 40) and why does faith involve suffering? (pp. 39–40)

5. Why did Paul include the Christ-hymn of 2:6-11? In your view, what is the major point the hymn makes a) about Christ and b) about Christian life? (pp. 41–44)

6. What is the nature of the debate behind Paul's harsh words and intense rhetoric in 3:2-11? For Paul what is the nature of the divine-human relationship? (pp. 46–48)

7. Euodia and Syntyche were important in Philippi but are hardly mentioned now. Why were they important and do we now appreciate their importance? (p. 50)

2 Thessalonians

1. What do you particularly like or dislike about this letter?

2. What do you think of the debate about authorship? What (if anything) persuades you that Paul did (not) write the letter? (pp. 53–57)

3. What does it mean to say that "the scriptures, though inspired, have their limitations" (p. 58)? What does sound interpretation of scripture always include? (pp. 58–59)

4. Given the complexities of interpreting 2:3-12, what should we make of those who claim that this text and others are about to be fulfilled in the 21st century?

5. How should we interpret the harsh and vengeful sections of this letter? (pp. 60, 64)

6. Expectation of the end is a common theme in this letter and elsewhere (e.g. 1 Thess 4:13-18; 1 Cor 7:29-31). What are the strengths and weaknesses of living with an awareness of the end of the world?

Colossians

1. What are the different meanings of "the church" in this letter? Contrast 1:18, 24 with 4:15 in this regard. How do these different emphases cohere? (p. 90)

2. In outline, what was "the philosophy" that the writer saw as a threat to the Colossian believers? Do analogous philosophies sometimes appear in Christianity today? (pp. 70, 76, 80–83)

3. What is the thrust of the letter's response to "the philosophy"? Is it relevant to our attitudes to religious law(s) of various types?

4. How does the hymn (1:15-20), especially its description of Christ and the Church, respond to "the philosophy"? (pp. 76–78)

5. Though the letter warns against "rules and regulations" (p. 82), it also lays down some "household rules" (pp. 86–87) that many today find problematic. How are these two parts of the letter to be balanced, and what do you make of 3:18-25?

6. What do we learn about baptism in this letter, and about the responsibility it involves for all the baptized to be "the Church"? (pp. 81–82, 85–86)

7. Why did some copiers change "her" to "his" in 4:15? Is it important for the Church today that there were women leaders in the early churches?

Ephesians

1. Part of the uniqueness of Ephesians is its focus on "the [universal] Church." Why is it valuable for believers in every generation to understand this universal (catholic) aspect of the Church and of faith? (p. 98)

2. When Ephesians was written there was no "clergy"; all, in different ways and degrees, had responsibility for ministry (4:12) and all ministers (4:11) were "lay" men and women. Is it important to bear this in mind for understanding the Church and ministry today? (pp. 93–94, 105–106)

3. What is the evidence that the writer had a high regard for Judaism? What is the significance of this for Christians in terms of their thinking about Judaism? (pp. 100–102)

4. Ephesians emphasizes the "presence" of salvation (e.g. 1:7; 2:4-8), but ultimately acknowledges that "the victory is not complete" (pp. 99, 116). What is the value, but also the danger, of emphasizing the *presence* of salvation now?

5. Why do you think the writer emphasizes so much that salvation is "God's gift, not a matter of [human] actions" (2:8-9)? And how are we to balance this with the further emphasis on believers' responsibility to do good? (p. 100)

6. Ephesians 5:21–6:9 is both problematic ("wives" and "slaves") and profound ("the mystery [of the marriage between] Christ and the Church"). What are we to make of this passage today?

7. How does Ephesians (perhaps more than any other New Testament book) support the belief that the Church is "one, holy, catholic and apostolic"? (e.g. p. 105)

INDEX OF CITATIONS FROM THE
CATECHISM OF THE CATHOLIC CHURCH

The arabic number(s) following the citation refer to the paragraph number(s) in the *Catechism of the Catholic Church.* The asterisk following a paragraph number indicates that the citation has been paraphrased.

1 Thessalonians

1:10	442*
2:13	104,* 1349*
2:14-15	597*
3:2	307
4:7	2518,* 2813
4:11	2427*
4:13-14	1012*
4:14	649, 989*
4:16	1001
4:17	1025*
4:18	1687*
5:2-3	675*
5:2	673*
5:5	1216
5:6	2849*
5:8	1820
5:12-13	1269*
5:17-18	2633*
5:17	1174, 2742, 2757
5:18	2638, 2648
5:19	696
5:23	367
5:25	2636*

Philippians

1:3-4	2636*
1:9-11	2632*
1:21	1010, 1698
1:23	1005, 1011, 1021,* 1025*

1:27	1692
2:1	2842*
2:4	2635
2:5-8	461
2:5	520,* 1694, 2842*
2:6-11	2641,* 2667*
2:6-9	1850*
2:6	449
2:7	472, 602,* 705,* 713, 876, 1224
2:8-9	908*
2:8	411, 612, 623
2:9-11	449,* 2812
2:9-10	434
2:10-11	201*
2:10	633,* 635
2:12-13	1949
2:13	308
2:14-17	1070*
2:15	1243*
2:25	1070*
2:30	1070*
3:6	752*
3:8-11	428
3:8	133
3:10-11	989,* 1006*
3:10	648*
3:20	1003,* 2796*
3:21	556, 999
4:6-7	2633*
4:8	1803

4:13	273,* 308,* 1460

2 Thessalonians

1:10	1041
1:11	2636*
2:3-12	673*
2:4-12	675*
2:7	385, 671*
3:6-13	2830*
3:10	2427

Colossians

1:3-6	2632*
1:3	2636*
1:10	2520*
1:12-14	1250*
1:13-14	517*
1:14	2839
1:15-20	2641*
1:15	241, 299, 381, 1701
1:16-17	291
1:16	331
1:18-20	624*
1:18	504,* 658, 753,* 792
1:20-22	2305*
1:24	307,* 618,* 1508
1:27	568, 772
2:9	484, 515, 722, 2502

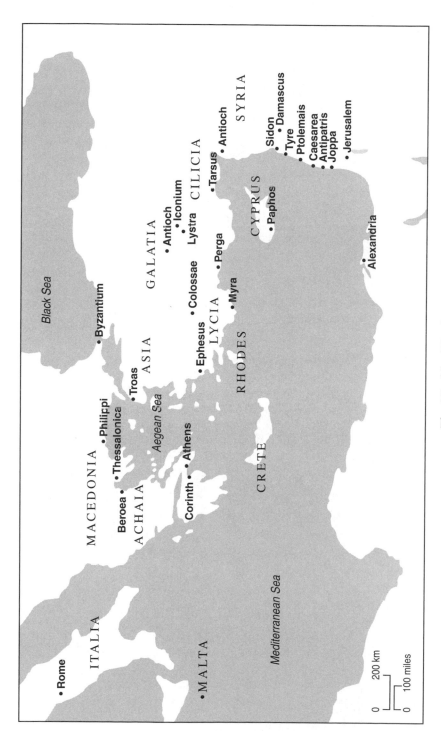

The World of Paul